# 5 HABITS OF HAPPY FAMILIES

## WES HAYSTEAD

Gospel Light

Gospel Light is an evangelical Christian publisher dedicated to serving the local church. We believe God's vision for Gospel Light is to provide church leaders with biblical, user-friendly materials that will help them evangelize, disciple and minister to children, youth and families.

We hope this Gospel Light resource will help you discover biblical truth for your own life and help you minister to adults. God bless you in your work.

*For a free catalog from Gospel Light please contact your Christian supplier or call* 1-800-4-GOSPEL.

**PUBLISHING STAFF**
**Jean Daly,** Editor
**Kyle Duncan,** Editorial Director
**Gary S. Greig, Ph.D.,** Editor in Chief

ISBN 0-8307-1716-1
© 1995 Gospel Light Publications
All rights reserved.
Printed in U.S.A.

# How to Make Clean Copies from This Book

**You may make copies of portions of this book with a clean conscience if:**

- you (or someone in your organization) are the original purchaser;
- you are using the copies you make for a noncommercial purpose (such as teaching or promoting your ministry) within your church or organization;
- you follow the instructions provided in this book.

**However, it is ILLEGAL for you to make copies if:**

- you are using the material to promote, advertise or sell a product or service other than for ministry fund-raising;
- you are using the material in or on a product for sale;
- you or your organization are **not** the original purchaser of this book.

By following these guidelines you help us keep our products affordable.

Thank you,

Gospel Light

# Contents

# How to Use *5 Habits of Happy Families*

## What This Course Is About

Everyone knows that families are facing big trouble. The continuing high rate of divorce is not just a set of disturbing statistics, nor even a major contributor to many of the deepest ills of modern society. However, fragmented and broken homes are a present reality that touch us all.

"Wouldn't it be great if we could turn back the clock," many of us often wish, "back to a time when families were strong and healthy?" While we know clocks only turn in one direction, it's understandable to sometimes yearn for a simpler, better time.

Sooner or later such a quest propels us back into Bible times, where we expect to find a host of strong, healthy families to admire and emulate. Surely, the writers of Scripture have left us many examples of how the great heroes of the faith lived out that faith at home. As we start to turn the pages of the Book, it doesn't take long for us to come face-to-face with a hard reality: The Bible presents far more examples of family failures than it does family successes. And each example shows that God's grace sustains and gives hope even in the worst family failures.

From the story of the very first couple disobeying God, the Bible recounts over and over again the terrible toll exacted on human families once sin entered our world. Repeatedly as we peer into the family lives of those giants of the faith, we are stunned to find, instead of paragons of virtue, men and women afflicted with the same weaknesses and failings that beset us.

The Bible does not portray ideal families, isolated from stress and conflict. Instead, with an often brutal reality, the Bible shows us that strong, healthy families have never been easy to build or maintain. Neither is family success unattainable. For, sprinkled through the stories of failures, we see God breaking through and bringing hope to fallible, failure-prone people who did achieve notable success in family living.

These biblical accounts are the focus of this course. Instead of dwelling on the failures, we have chosen to explore the successes. Without ignoring the reality of problems, this course examines five important keys God gives us for building and maintaining quality relationships. These keys make a big difference in any personal relationship, but within the close confines of a family, these keys are vital:

- Respect
- Resolving Conflict
- Commitment
- Communication
- God's Family

As you and your group explore each key, the real-life illustration from Scripture will help connect that concept to the everyday world of living in a family.

# Introduction

## It's Your Choice in Using *5 Habits of Happy Families*

This exciting study of successful family living has been designed to fit a variety of learning situations:

- You have a choice of course length (5 to 10 sessions);
- You have a choice of session plans (from 60 to 90 minutes);
- You have a choice of settings (classroom or home), meeting times (Sunday mornings, Sunday evenings, weekdays or evenings) and frequency (once a week, every day or night, weekend retreat);
- You have a choice of age-group structures (adults alone or adults linked to children's and youth groups).

Whenever or wherever you can get a group of people together to explore biblical guidance for successful families, this resource will be an invaluable guide.

## This Leader's Guide

*5 Habits of Happy Families* is a unique resource, offering a stimulating and enjoyable opportunity for group study of successful family living.

This leader's guide is unique because it:

- offers the flexibility of completing this study in either 5 or 10 sessions;
- is based on the premise that a study of biblical insights for family living is a truly exciting adventure with great value for everyone: parents, singles, grandparents, men and women.
- explores five biblical examples of individuals living out principles of healthy family living;
- provides useful handles for helping people see the personal implications of the biblical examples studied;
- includes proven strategies for enjoyable group interaction, enabling people to learn from the experiences of others;
- references the *SonTown Family Celebration* course for children, an innovative parallel study that allows all family members to explore the same biblical content in ways appropriate to various levels of development;
- requires very few additional supplies for class sessions (An overhead projector is helpful, but not necessary. Blank paper, index cards, pencils and felt markers are typical of the easily secured materials that help add variety and stimulate involvement. Suggested supplies are listed at the beginning of each session.);
- suggests family-interaction assignments to follow each session, adding further reinforcement to each family member's learning.

## Session Plan

Each of the five sessions is flexibly designed to be completed in one of three major time schedules:

Option A—Five sessions of 60-75 minutes each.

Option B—Five sessions of more than 75 minutes each.

Option C—Ten sessions of 60 minutes each.

Two important symbols are used in the session plans to aid in extending each session over two separate meetings.

This symbol indicates the Two-Meeting Track that allows you to extend the session over two meetings, giving group members more time for discussion. The stop-and-go sign means to END your first meeting and BEGIN your second meeting at the point where the symbol appears in the session plan. Each of the 5 sessions in this resource can thus be easily made into 2 complete meetings, for a total of 10 sessions (Option C).

You will find instructions placed in boxes and marked with this clock symbol. This information provides optional learning experiences to extend this session over two meetings or to accommodate a session longer than 60-75 minutes (Options B or C).

# Sample Session Plan

## Getting Started

### (10 minutes)

Each session begins with a choice of two relationship-building, family-sharing activities that also help group members begin thinking of the main truth of the session.

### Getting Started Option

This option will add 10 minutes to the Getting Started section, either reviewing highlights of the previous session or further introducing the current session.

## Getting into the Word

### (40 minutes)

Each session contains three to five major points, enabling class members to recall the biblical narrative and the implications for family living today. For example:

### Step 1—First Point (15 minutes)

Complete instructions are given to enable the teacher to guide class members in helpful and enjoyable learning experiences.

### Option

This option will add five minutes to the Step 1 section. These optional activities explore aspects of each main point that could not be addressed in the shorter time schedules.

# Introduction

Note: If you are completing this session in one meeting, ignore this break and continue with next step.

Two-Meeting Track: If you want to spread this session over two meetings, STOP here and close in prayer. Inform group members of the content to be covered in your next meeting.

## Start Option (10 minutes)

Begin your second meeting by reviewing the main ideas from the first half of the session. (Suggested review activities are in each session.)

# Getting Personal

## (10 minutes)

Each session concludes with instruction and questions for summarizing session highlights, helping people make personal application of a main truth, plus suggestions for family interaction at home.

## Getting Personal Option

This option adds five minutes to Getting Personal, probing one personal issue studied.

# A Few Teaching Tips

### 1. Keep It Simple.

The Bible contains a vast amount of highly interesting, deeply meaningful information. Avoid trying to pass all this information on to your eager learners. They will remember far more if you keep the focus on the Key Idea of each session.

### 2. Keep It Light.

Some of the introductory activities in this resource are fun! This is intentional. Many people who most need this course are intimidated by the topic of successful family living. Often there is fear that their inadequacies will be exposed. People who are intimidated and fearful are not ready to learn. The light-hearted approaches are devices to help people relax so they can learn efficiently.

### 3. Keep It Significant.

Because this course has some light touches does not mean its content can be handled frivolously. Keep clearly in mind—and repeatedly emphasize with your class—that this course is dealing with the major keys to successful family living. The insights gained in these sessions can make a big difference in every family represented in your group.

### 4. Keep It Interactive.

The learning activities in this resource provide a variety of involving experiences, recognizing the various learning styles that will be present in any group of adults. While some of the activities may not fit your preferred teaching style, by using this varied path to learning, you make sure that those who learn differently than you do will have their needs met. A common type of involvement is using the Bible—locating, reading and talking about selected passages. If you have people in your group who are unfamiliar with the locations of Bible books, your patient encouragement will help them make the exciting discovery that they really can study the Bible. If you have people in your group who do not have Bibles, provide Bibles for them.

### 5. Keep It Prayerful.

Both in your preparation and in each class session, pray earnestly that you and your class will learn what God wants you to learn and that His Spirit will give you wisdom as you prepare to lead the session.

# Linking with *SonTown Family Celebration*

If you are teaching this class in conjunction with a children's program using the *SonTown Family Celebration* course materials, you won't need to make any significant modification in the session plans in this resource. The children involved in *SonTown Family Celebration* will be studying the same biblical principles and examples, enabling family members to enjoy comparing notes on what they learned in their separate sessions.

1. *SonTown Family Celebration* provides an opportunity to do at least a part of each session with families together as a unit. Instructions for this option are provided in the *SonTown Family Celebration Intergenerational VBS Guide*.

2. Whether or not your group actually meets at all with the children in *SonTown Family Celebration*, alert the parents in your group to ways they can take advantage of this unique all-family learning opportunity. For example:

- Alert parents that after every session their children will bring home a colorful publication summarizing the key points they studied, and with helpful suggestions for family interaction;

- Encourage parents to share something they learned (or were reminded of) BEFORE asking their children to talk about what they learned;

- Explain that the issue is not how much Bible information a person knows, but what we do with what we know and whether or not we grow close to Christ. Challenge participants to use the family interaction ideas for each session.

To capture the interest of people in this course:

- Share some of your own experiences of finding the Bible relevant to contemporary family problems. To succeed in leading this course, you do not need to have resolved all family problems. You do need to be honest about some of your struggles in seeking to live out God's intention for healthy families;

- Point out that while societies and cultures change, God and His Word have remained constant over centuries and across continents. This course deals with principles that are at the core of human relationships, thus they have as much value today as they did when the Bible was written;

- Allow people to talk about their own family experiences. This study is not a therapy session, but there is significant learning value as people tell each other of real-life experiences related to the key idea being studied;

- Instruct group members to be sensitive about the privacy of family members. When a group of parents gets together, there is a great temptation to "tell all" about their children. While sharing with other parents is helpful, there is sometimes a fine line between helpful sharing and destructive gossip.

# RESPECT: Noah's Family Works Together

## SESSION KEYS

### Key Verses

"Honor your father and your mother, as the LORD your God has commanded you." Deuteronomy 5:16

"Fathers, do not exasperate your children; instead, bring them up in the training and instruction of the Lord." Ephesians 6:4

### Key Idea

Successful families follow the Lord's direction to respect, trust and appreciate one another.

### Key Readings

Genesis 6:5—8:5,13-20; 9:18-27

## PREPARATION

"It really bothers me," a parent confided to a friend, "to hear how Nancy and Phil's boys talk to them. They don't show any respect at all."

"Well," the friend replied, "that's pretty much how Nancy and Phil talk to the boys."

Children learn respect, not so much by being told to respect, as by being given respect themselves. When Paul wrote to Timothy, he urged leaders in the church to see that their own children obey them "with proper respect" (1 Tim. 3:4). At first glance, this appears to indicate that children can be coerced into respecting parents. However, Paul wisely gave this instruction only after listing the qualities ("temperate, self-controlled, respectable,...gentle, not quarrelsome" [vv. 2,3]) that make a person deserving of respect.

However, what is a child—or anyone—to do when a person in authority does not display all these fine qualities? Rather than using a person's failings as an excuse to be disrespectful, we need to look for all that is good and healthy in the other person. It is relatively easy to show respect to someone we readily admire. It is much more of a challenge to show respect to someone we know is imperfect. Noah's family provides a good example of family members working together. While others may have ridiculed Noah, his family stood by him, and they all benefited.

This session will help your class members identify qualities they admire in the members of their families. They will also explore practical ways to communicate respect for others, treating family members as unique, special people, created by God, and worthy of being treated respectfully.

Provide blank name tags and felt-tip pens. Make a tag for yourself.

On a table at the front of the room, provide materials for one of these Getting Started choices:

Choice 1: A large sheet of butcher paper (long enough to extend across one wall) and felt-tip pens. Either mount the paper on a wall, spread it across two or more tables, or spread it on the floor across the front or back of the room. Across the top of the paper, letter, "A Forest of Family Trees." At one end of the paper, sketch your family tree, showing your parents and grandparents as the roots, you and your spouse as the trunk, and your children as the branches. Add each child's current age. Use both your name and your spouse's name to label the tree (i.e., "The Smith/Jones Family Tree"). Add three or four "fruit" to the tree, labeling each with an area of interest shared by most (or at least some) of your family members (i.e., "Sports," "Country Music," "Cats," etc.). Distribute felt-tip pens around the paper.

Choice 2: Make an overhead transparency of "Family Profile" on page 25. Secure an overhead projector and focus it at the front of the room. Slide a sheet of paper under the "Family Profile" transparency so that only the heading and the first incomplete statement are showing.

Also have ready large sheets of blank paper (one sheet per four to five people) and felt-tip pens.

On each of the four walls, mount a strip of butcher paper or shelf paper. Letter each of these four headings, one on each strip: "Parents show disrespect when...," "Kids show disrespect when...," "Husbands/Wives show disrespect when..." and "Disrespect hurts...." Letter the text of Ephesians 6:4 on a poster and mount it at the front of the room.

On each of six sheets of poster board, letter a different synonym for respect: "Respect," "Honor," "Admire," "Trust," "Appreciate" and "Value." Mount the six posters around the room.

Duplicate on bright colored paper a copy of "To My Family..." on page 27 for each participant.

# Session 1 at a Glance

| SECTION | ONE-SESSION PLAN | | TWO-SESSION PLAN | WHAT YOU'LL DO |
|---|---|---|---|---|
| | 60 to 75 Minutes | More than 75 Minutes | 60 Minutes (each session) | |
| Getting Started | 10 | 10-20 | Session One: 20 | Get Acquainted— Introduce Family Issues |
| Getting into the Word | 40 | 60-75 | 40 | Explore Value of Respect in Families |
| Step 1 | 15 | 20 | 20 | Marks of Disrespect |
| Step 2 | 15 | 20 | 20 | Noah's Family: Respect and Disrespect |
| | | | Session Two Start Option: 10 | Qualities Deserving Respect |
| Step 3 | 10 | 20 | 20 | My Family Needs Me to Respect |
| (Step 4 Option) | (15) | (15) | 15 | Ways to Show Respect |
| Getting Personal | 10 | 10-15 | 15 | Letters to Families |

# Session Plan

## Leader's Choice

**Two-Meeting Track:** This session is designed to be completed in one 60- to 75-minute meeting. If you want to extend the session over two meetings and allow group members more time for discussion, **END** your first meeting and **BEGIN** your second meeting at the stop-and-go symbol in the session plan.

The boxes marked with the clock symbol provide optional learning experiences to extend this session over two meetings or to accommodate a session longer than 60-75 minutes.

# Getting Started

## (10 minutes)

### Choice 1—Family Trees

Welcome people as they arrive and guide them to make and wear name tags. To help people begin to get acquainted and build relationships, invite them to sketch a tree on the butcher paper, following the example you provided. Couples should work together. Encourage people to introduce themselves to one another as they observe each other's trees, noting families with similar numbers and ages of children.

As the final touches are being put on the trees, invite volunteers to share something interesting they learned from another family's tree. Give an example or two to help people get started: **I had never known that Sarah Garcia's last name used to be Bangs. Maybe we're related. And I was intrigued to see the Mattia tree decorated with a nice, large fruit labeled "Gardening." I could sure use some help in my backyard, Larry.**

### Choice 2—Family Profiles

Welcome people as they arrive and guide them to make and wear name tags. Use the overhead projector to project "Family Profile" onto the screen or a wall. Read aloud the instructions at the top of the screen. **To help us start thinking about successful family living, and get to know each other a little better, introduce yourself to someone from a different family and tell each other how you would complete the following statements.** Allow about one minute for people to find partners and each complete the first statement: **"The family I grew up in...."**

Instruct everyone to find a new partner and each complete the second statement: **"My family today...."** Again, allow about one minute for people to find new partners and complete the statement. As time allows, continue similarly with the remaining statements.

Conclude this Getting Started activity by inviting volunteers to share one interesting thing they learned about someone else's family experiences.

### Getting Started Option: The Family in the Bible

This option will add 10 minutes to the Getting Started section.

Invite people to form at least four groups of no more than four to six members per group. (If you have fewer than eight people, just form two groups.) Ask one person from each group to pick up a sheet of paper and two or three felt-tip pens from the supply table. Then divide the room into four sections, giving the group(s) in each section these topics:

Section 1: Old Testament examples of successful family living
Section 2: Old Testament examples of family problems

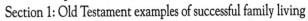

Section 3: New Testament examples of successful family living

Section 4: New Testament examples of family problems

(If you have just two groups, assign one group to consider successful examples and the other group to work on examples of family problems.)

Instruct the groups to list on his or her sheet of paper all the examples he or she can think of that fit their assigned topic. Encourage them to think of both husband/wife and parent/child relationships. Allow about five minutes for groups to work.

Ask someone in each group to hold up his or her list while another group member reads off the examples he or she listed, telling what happened that was either successful or created problems. It will probably be obvious that the Bible has more examples of family problems than successes. Ask group members to suggest reasons why this might be so. Possible explanations might include:

• The Bible is an accurate record of human experience and, since the Fall, all areas of human life have been damaged.

• Stories of failures tend to be more interesting to us than stories of successes. (This is probably not a reason such accounts were included, but may help explain why most people are more familiar with the problem accounts than with the positive ones.)

• It is encouraging to know we're not the only ones who face struggles at home. Even the giants of biblical history had domestic problems.

• We can learn from other people's mistakes, helping us to avoid the same pitfalls.

As time permits, invite volunteers to share one thing they have learned about family living from the problems or successes recorded in Scripture.

# Getting into the Word

## (40 minutes)

### Step 1—Marks of Disrespect (15 minutes)

Introduce this study by commenting, **In this course, we will focus on five family relationships that illustrate important principles of successful family living. These are positive examples that we can all follow in our own family relationships. Today we are going to look at a family that showed respect when it probably wasn't easy. To help us get a feel for why respect is so vital within a family, I want everyone to get up and go over by the nearest wall and group around the poster about disrespect.** (If one group ends up significantly larger than others, ask a few people to move to another group. If the groups are too large for easy conversation—more than six or eight people—have them form two or more smaller groups.)

When the groups have been formed, give these instructions. **Disrespect comes in many forms. One of the most visible signs of disrespect in our society is graffiti—**

*— next week*

*> we are going to...*

*as groups*

writing or drawing that defaces someone else's property. Right now, I'm giving you permission to create some graffiti, writing on your poster about disrespect within the family. Talk with your group about some ways to complete your poster's statement about disrespect. As you think of ideas, send someone to the poster to write that idea in big bold letters. You have about five minutes to see how much graffiti you can create about disrespect in the family.

When groups seem to be running low on further ideas, call time and invite people to return to their seats. Ask for a representative from each group to read aloud the graffiti they wrote about disrespect, saving the "Disrespect hurts..." poster for last. As the graffiti is read, ask a few questions to help the group analyze the ideas being shared. A few examples:

How common are those evidences of disrespect in families today?

What happens in a family when disrespect is shown?

Why are children so vulnerable to being hurt by others' disrespect?

How are children hurt when they are disrespectful of others?

Then summarize: We've used graffiti as a tangible example of disrespect, that at its core is any action or attitude that puts self above others. We've identified some examples of disrespect within families today, and we've considered the harmful results of disrespect on individuals and the family.

## Option

This option will add five minutes to the Step 1 section.

Invite volunteers to locate and read aloud the following proverbs about "mockers"—people who do not show respect to others:

Proverbs 3:34

Proverbs 21:24

Proverbs 24:8,9

Comment: Lack of respect for others is not simply a mark of poor manners. It is a cancerous, sinful flaw that damages a person as well as all his or her relationships with other people. Lack of respect within a family is therefore of grave concern because of the continuing, deep-seated injuries it inflicts. In contrast, when family members show respect to one another, everyone flourishes.

## Step 2—Noah's Family: Respect and Disrespect (15 minutes)

Introduce the study of Noah's family: In the Genesis account of the Flood, the focus is on Noah and his obedience to God. But there were seven other people very deeply involved in this endeavor who should not be overlooked: Noah's family members. We get our first real introduction to Noah's family in a very remarkable passage that contrasts Noah and his family from the surrounding society.

Ask for eight volunteers to each read aloud a verse from Genesis 6. Assign each volunteer a verse, starting with verse 5 and ending with verse 12. Have those reading

verses 5-7 and 11-12 (descriptions of society in Noah's day) line up at one side of the room. Those reading verses 8 and 9 (description of Noah) line up along the other side. The one reading verse 10 stands in the middle. Signal the readers to begin, each reading the assigned verse in order.

When the reading is finished, gesture to the readers on either side and comment: **The contrast between Noah and the rest of society is vividly drawn. But what about Noah's family? What side did they line up on? Did they identify with their friends and peers or with their 600-year-old father? Interestingly, nowhere does the Bible come right out and say that Noah's family took a stand with Noah. But let's take a look at some things it does say.**

Ask for other volunteers to read aloud these verses:
Genesis 6:22—7:1
Genesis 7:5-7
Genesis 7:11,12
Genesis 7:23
Genesis 8:15,16
Genesis 8:18
Genesis 9:1
Genesis 9:8,9

After the readings are completed, comment: **Notice the linkage repeated throughout the whole story: Noah obeyed God and his family was with him. Over and over again we see it. Noah's family members weren't just passengers along for the ride. They were vital companions and supporters through the whole process, and were not just saved from the flood with Noah, but they were specifically included in God's blessing and covenant.**

Now, **what does this have to do with the issue of respect? The word is never used in the whole story.** Invite responses from the group. If necessary, point out that the entire narrative is a powerful illustration of respect. There is no evidence that Noah's family ever heard any of God's instructions to Noah. All they had to go on was Noah's word, backed up by his character. **In the face of any doubts about constructing a huge boat on dry land, of gathering vast quantities of food for animals they had never seen, of discounting the disbelief (and probable scoffing) of all their friends and neighbors, Noah's family members showed their respect for him in the most practical terms possible: they worked alongside him.**

Engage the group in considering the implications of the respect shown by Noah's family. Ask the following questions:

**What would have happened if Noah's family had not respected him?** (Obviously, they would not have believed him and would probably have refused to assist him in such a far-fetched project.)

**From what you know of Noah, what do you think he had done to earn his family's respect?** (Besides living a long time in a society that valued longevity,

Genesis 6:9 says, "Noah was a righteous man, blameless among the people of his time, and he walked with God." Now there is someone worth respecting!)

Summarize: **The picture we get of Noah's relationship with his family is never one of him cajoling or pleading for the respect he deserved. Instead, we see a man who carefully nurtured a right relationship with God and consistently sought to do right toward other people. His character earned respect.**

If time permits, read aloud these New Testament statements about Noah to reinforce the point that his character and life earned respect:

Hebrews 11:7 (He was a man of faith and reverence—"holy fear.")

2 Peter 2:5 (He was a preacher—literally, a "herald"—of righteousness; he had a reputation for speaking what was right and true.)

## Option

This option will add five minutes to the Step 2 section.

Point out that Scripture never tries to paint Noah or his family as perfect. The Genesis 9 account of his drunkenness and the lack of respect shown by Ham is a sobering reminder that even the best of families are subject to human failures—sin. While our attention seems to be drawn to the failings of Noah and Ham, it is important to call attention to the great act of respect by Shem and Japheth in covering their father's nakedness.

Ask **What are some times family members need to show respect for another by not calling attention to that person's failings?** (Disciplining or reprimanding a family member should be done privately, not in public, if at all possible. "Cute" or embarrassing stories of things a family member did should not be told outside the family.)

Comment: **Respect does not require perfection. It is a recognition that the other person has worth and value, and deserves to be treated as such. This does not mean that a family member should be allowed to abuse another and hide behind the cloak of family secrecy.**

**Note:** If you are completing this session in one meeting, ignore this break and continue with Step 3.

**Two-Meeting Track:** If you want to spread this session over two meetings, **STOP** here and close in prayer. Inform group members of the content to be covered in your next meeting.

## Start Option (10 minutes)

Before your second meeting, draw vertical lines about 24 inches apart on the chalkboard or a large sheet of butcher paper mounted on a wall. Across the top of the board or paper, letter "Qualities I Respect in My Child." As everyone arrives, invite each to write his or her child's name in one of the columns, listing one or more qualities he or she respects in that child.

When the board or paper has numerous entries, invite people to be seated. To review the main ideas from the first half of the session, ask volunteers to share reasons why mutual respect is so important in a family. Then continue with Step 3 and conclude the session.

## Step 3—My Family Needs Me to Respect... (10 minutes)

Refer to the poster of Ephesians 6:4. Lead the group in reading it aloud in unison. Ask **Does this instruction apply to mothers as well as fathers?** (Obviously.) **What linkage do you see between this instruction and the command to children, quoted immediately before this verse, to honor parents?** (Honor—or respect—of parents grows out of parents' treatment of children. The parent who continually exasperates—provokes, irritates, nags, angers or, in other words, does not treat with respect—a child, actually keeps that child from learning to respect. Respect is definitely a two-way street.)

Call attention to the six posters around the room, each with a different word expressing the idea of respect. Divide the class into six sections. (If any section has six or more people, have them form smaller groups of three or four members each. If you have fewer than 12 people total, form three groups.) Assign each section one of the six words. (If you have three groups, assign each group two words.) Instruct groups to describe to each other evidence they have observed that their children need that particular quality from them. **What have you seen in your child's behavior and attitudes that indicates he or she needs appreciation or trust, or to be valued by you?** As groups talk, letter boldly across the chalkboard this message based on Ephesians 6:4: "Fathers and mothers, _____ your children so that you may bring them up in the training and instruction of the Lord."

Conclude the group sharing by leading the class in reading aloud in unison the message you have written, with each group in turn as you point to them, stating the quality they have just discussed. Thus, the message will sound like this:

All: "Fathers and mothers,

Section 1: "respect,"

Section 2: "honor,"

Section 3: "admire,"

Section 4: "trust,"

Section 5: "appreciate,"

Section 6: "value"

All: "your children so that you may bring them up in the training and instruction of the Lord."

Repeat once or twice for emphasis.

## Option

This option will add 10 minutes to the Step 3 section.

Ask **When is it most difficult for a parent to show these qualities of respect to a child?** (When tired or irritable; when children disobey; when normal child behaviors conflict with adult desires, etc.)

Ask **What can a parent do at such times to avoid responding to children in ways that exasperate?** Be prepared to suggest a few ideas such as: **Pray before reacting; remind yourself to consider the child's perspective; avoid responses that attack the child** ("You are so [thoughtless, lazy, annoying, etc.]!"); **clearly state how you feel about the situation** ("I feel like you don't try to listen to me."); **seek to include the child in resolving the problem, rather than simply imposing a punishment** ("What do you think we could do to improve this?").

## Step 4 Option—Ways to Show Respect (15 minutes)

Ask volunteers to suggest specific ways parents can show respect for children. List ideas on a blank overhead transparency or on the chalkboard. As each example is suggested, ask others in the group to comment on how that action or attitude will benefit the child and/or the family.

After a variety of examples have been listed, ask volunteers to suggest specific ways parents can show respect for each other to their children. As ideas are shared, ask questions such as **Why is it important for children to see respect between both parents? How does this apply in the case of divorced or separated parents? What are some ways a parent might unwittingly convey to children a lack of respect for a spouse?**

Finally, ask **How do we show respect when a family member has done something that is not deserving of respect?** (It is important to distinguish between respecting the person and accepting whatever that person may do. Unacceptable behavior, whether by a child or an adult, cannot be allowed to continue. Dealing honestly and openly with a person's responsibility to do what is right is essential for treating a person with full respect.)

# Getting Personal
## (10 minutes)

Distribute copies of "To My Family...." Provide pens or pencils to those who need one. Give these instructions: **Write a private letter to your family. Choose one of three approaches to the letter, that you may choose to read to them or save as a personal reminder for yourself.**

**Option 1:** Tell each person some qualities that have earned your respect and that you thank God for.

**Option 2:** Confess times you have not shown the respect you should.

**Option 3:** Describe some of the ways you can ask the Lord to help you show more respect toward each family member.

### Getting Personal Option

This option will add five minutes to the Getting Personal section.

Form groups of no more than four or five people. Invite each person to read aloud one thing he or she wrote. Hearing what others in similar situations are doing is often helpful. Stress that some people may have written things that should be kept within their own families, and that right to privacy should be respected. Suggest that those who prefer not to share any part of their letters simply tell what they intend to do with them.

Close in prayer.

Announce that the next session will focus on how God wants us to resolve conflict within families.

 # Family Profile

## Welcome!

To help us start thinking about successful family living, and get to know each other a little better, introduce yourself to someone from a different family and tell each other how you would complete the following statements:

**1. The family I grew up in...**

.............................................................................................

.............................................................................................

**2. My family today...**

.............................................................................................

.............................................................................................

**3. My favorite family pet...**

.............................................................................................

.............................................................................................

**4. One family member I always admired...**

.............................................................................................

.............................................................................................

**5. Respect is important in a family because...**

.............................................................................................

.............................................................................................

**6. I think family members learn to respect others by...**

.............................................................................................

.............................................................................................

# "To My Family..."

"To My Family..."

........................................................................................................

........................................................................................................

........................................................................................................

........................................................................................................

........................................................................................................

........................................................................................................

........................................................................................................

........................................................................................................

........................................................................................................

........................................................................................................

........................................................................................................

........................................................................................................

........................................................................................................

........................................................................................................

........................................................................................................

........................................................................................................

........................................................................................................

........................................................................................................

........................................................................................................

........................................................................................................

........................................................................................................

........................................................................................................

........................................................................................................

........................................................................................................

........................................................................................................

# Resolving Conflict: Jacob and Esau Forgive

## Session Keys

### Key Verses

"Why do you look at the speck of sawdust in your brother's eye and pay no attention to the plank in your own eye? How can you say to your brother, 'Let me take the speck out of your eye,' when all the time there is a plank in your own eye? You hypocrite, first take the plank out of your own eye, and then you will see clearly to remove the speck from your brother's eye." Matthew 7:3-5

"Bear with each other and forgive whatever grievances you may have against one another. Forgive as the Lord forgave you." Colossians 3:13

### Key Idea

Successful families follow the Lord's direction to resolve conflicts by practicing mutual forgiveness, not retribution.

### Key Readings

Genesis 25:21-34; 32; 33

## Preparation

Conflict occurs in all families. Whenever two or more human beings live together, there will be occasions for disagreements, misunderstandings, rivalries—resulting in disappointment, frustration, anger and jealousy—and sometimes it seems as if those are the good days.

The reality of conflict within families is readily apparent, both in real life and in the pages of Scripture. The Bible is an intensely honest and practical book. It never shies away from the sometimes harsh realities of human experiences. Neither does it dangle impossible goals in front of us, telling us to pursue courses of action that are doomed to failure.

In its numerous accounts of family conflicts, the Bible clearly shows us practical ways to avoid or reduce friction in family living. In the story of Jacob and Esau, we learn from the unfortunate examples of a family that let itself be torn apart. We also see in Jacob's elaborate preparations for his reunion with Esau, and Esau's willingness to accept Jacob's offerings, that there are practical actions that help reconcile the deep hurts that can divide family members. For example, we see the value in:

1. Taking the initiative in communication (see Gen. 32:3-6);
2. Identifying the conflict or problem (see Gen. 32:11);
3. Praying about the problem (see Gen. 32:9);
4. Seeing the other person's perspective (see Gen. 32:20);

5. Telling how you feel (see Gen. 33:3,4);
6. Taking action to correct the problem:
   - Make restitution (see Gen. 33:10,11);
   - Offer forgiveness and acceptance instead of seeking to get even or ahead (see Gen. 33:4,10,11).

The Genesis account does not provide a simple formula that guarantees results. It does provide a very honest example that can be useful for any family whose members prayerfully seek to resolve their grievances.

Provide blank name tags and felt-tip pens. Make a tag for yourself.

On a table at the front of the room, provide materials for this Getting Started choice if you will use the activity with your group:

Choice 1: Sheets of newsprint (one for every four to six people) and felt-tip pens.

On each of six large cards, letter one of the following references:

1. Genesis 32:3-6
2. Genesis 32:11
3. Genesis 32:9
4. Genesis 32:20
5. Genesis 33:3,4
6. Genesis 33:4,10,11

Make a transparency of "Actions that Help Resolve Conflict" on page 39.

Duplicate on bright-colored paper copies of "Oops! Pardon Me!" on page 41. Complete a copy for yourself so you can share one or two examples to help group members get started in completing their copies.

Letter three signs: "Forgive," "Excuse" and "Condone."

# Session 2 at a Glance

| SECTION | ONE-SESSION PLAN | | TWO-SESSION PLAN | WHAT YOU'LL DO |
|---|---|---|---|---|
| | 60 to 75 Minutes | More than 75 Minutes | 60 Minutes (each session) | |
| Getting Started | 10 | 10-20 | Session One: 20 | Introduce Resolving Conflict |
| Getting into the Word | 40 | 60-75 | 40 | Explore Causes and Resolutions of Family Conflicts |
| Step 1 | 15 | 20 | 20 | Setting Brother Against Brother |
| Step 2 | 15 | 20 | 20 | Jacob's Road to Reconciliation |
| | | | Session Two Start Option: 10 | The Gift of Peaceful Resolution |
| Step 3 | 10 | 20 | 20 | Teaching Forgiveness |
| (Step 4 Option) | (15) | (15) | 15 | Letting Go of a Grudge |
| Getting Personal | 10 | 10-15 | 15 | Writing Acts of Forgiveness |

# Session Plan

## Leader's Choice

**Two-Meeting Track:** This session is designed to be completed in one 60- to 75-minute meeting. If you want to extend the session over two meetings and allow group members more time for discussion, END your first meeting and BEGIN your second meeting at the stop-and-go symbol in the session plan.

The boxes marked with the clock symbol provide optional learning experiences to extend this session over two meetings or to accommodate a session longer than 60-75 minutes.

# Getting Started

## (10 minutes)

### Choice 1—Sources of Conflict

Welcome people as they arrive and guide them to complete and wear name tags. Have people form groups of four to six members. Provide each group with a sheet of newsprint and marking pen. Instruct the groups that, to introduce a potentially heavy topic with a light touch, they are to write words to a familiar tune describing some of the typical conflicts that occur in their families. Be prepared to sing a verse or two of a ditty about your family as an example (i.e., to the tune of "Old MacDonald Had a Farm": "Bob and Janet had some kids, ee-i, ee-i-o. And oh the things that those kids did, ee-i, ee-i-o. 'Stay out of my room!' 'He got a bigger piece!' Here a fight, there a gripe, everywhere an argument. Bob and Janet had some kids, ee-i, ee-i-o!").

Other tunes groups may consider: "Happy Birthday to You"; "Michael, Row the Boat Ashore"; "Mary Had a Little Lamb" and "Nobody Knows the Trouble I've Seen."

Allow about five minutes for groups to write their words, then invite each group to perform.

Point out that this session will focus on resolving conflicts within the family.

### Choice 2

Welcome people as they arrive and guide them to complete and wear name tags. Have people form groups of four to six members. Point out that every family faces conflicts, and sometimes we handle them well, and sometimes our best-intentioned efforts only seem to make matters worse (especially if there are teenagers in the house). To begin thinking about ways to resolve conflict, each person is to tell his or her group of a time when that person feels he or she handled a family conflict well, and of a time that person wishes he or she had handled it better. Set a pattern for this sharing by briefly telling two examples of your own—the more recent, the better. Your willingness to admit a time when you "blew it" will make it easier for other parents to be open about their shortcomings, thus preparing the group for the study to follow.

Conclude the group sharing by asking for a show of hands of those who remembered an incident they wish they had handled differently. How many recalled an incident they resolved well? Ask **Which incident was easier to recall?** (More people are likely to remember the times they "lost it" than the times they succeeded.) Comment: **Resolving conflicts within the family are among the most difficult challenges we face. Today we will explore some ways to help ourselves and our family members bury the resentments that often build up when conflicts do occur.**

## Getting Started Option: Family Conflicts in the Bible

This option will add 10 minutes to the Getting Started section.

Across the top of the chalkboard or a blank overhead transparency, letter "Family Conflicts in the Bible." Lead the group in compiling a list of incidents recorded in Scripture when there were interpersonal conflicts involving family members. Ask people to suggest incidents (i.e., Cain and Abel, Jacob and Esau, Joseph and his brothers, David and Absalom, etc.). Write the incidents on the chalkboard or overhead.

When the group starts to run out of ideas, ask **Which of these conflicts were successfully (peacefully) resolved?** Make a check mark in front of any that the group members mention. Most likely, there will be more incidents that are not checked than ones that are. Ask **Does it seem to you that conflicts among family members are more or less difficult to resolve than conflicts outside the family? Why?** Invite ideas from as many group members as time allows. Then comment: **Whether or not conflicts within a family are harder to resolve than those outside the family, there is ample evidence, both in Scripture and in our own experiences, that conflicts between family members have the potential to cause a great deal of lasting harm. This session will explore some helpful principles for successfully resolving conflicts within our families.**

# Getting into the Word
## (40 minutes)

### Step 1—Setting Brother Against Brother (15 minutes)

Introduce the story of Jacob and Esau: Of all the family conflicts recorded in Scripture, none is more intriguing or more instructive than the sibling rivalry between Jacob and his twin brother, Esau. The family experiences of Isaac and Rebekah are well worth our attention, both for the cautions they raise about some of the ways parents may contribute to problems among our offspring, as well as for noting some effective strategies God shows us in the account for mending fences that may sometimes seem hopelessly broken down.

Read aloud Genesis 25:21-28, instructing group members to look for a major danger signal of future conflict. Participants should point out the statement in verse 28 indicating Isaac's and Rebekah's favoritism. Comment: **Notice how something very positive—love—has the potential to stir up trouble. We are never told that Isaac or Rebekah hated, or even disliked, the other twin. But we clearly see the beginning of a lifelong split in this family caused by the parents choosing up sides, with each favoring a different brother. In chapter 27 we see the culmination of this pattern in Rebekah's plot to gain the blessing for Jacob at Esau's expense. Her decep-**

tion succeeded, but at a terrible price. The family was fragmented, her beloved Jacob was forced to flee from home, and she never saw him again.

Ask **What are some problems that tend to result when parents show favoritism?** (Resentment and competition among siblings, lack of self-esteem in the less-favored child, unfair treatment resulting in children becoming manipulative and selfish, lots of Smothers Brothers jokes about "Mother always loved you best," etc.)

After participants have had a chance to share ideas, comment: **Obviously, we're all totally fair and objective parents who would never dream of inflicting such damage on our children. Still, when we step** back and examine our feelings, we all find ourselves, at least from time to time, being drawn more toward one child than to others.

Ask **What are some actions that may indicate that parents are favoring one child over another?** (Comparing performance with statements such as, "Why can't you be more like your sister/brother?"; affirming one child's efforts or interests in some activity more than the other child's efforts or interests in another; accepting one child's ideas, suggestions or complaints more readily than those of the other child; spending more time with one child; seeking to "balance" the other parent's perceived favoritism.)

Point out that no one can be perfectly impartial, but parents need to be aware of the natural tendency to use favoritism, seeking honestly to provide each child with his or her fair measure of attention, affection and discipline.

## Option

This option will add five minutes to the Step 1 section.

Invite group members to share advice they might give Isaac and Rebekah. Ask **What would you suggest to help these parents deal with the resentment and competition between Jacob and Esau that was at least partly the result of Isaac and Rebekah playing favorites?** After several ideas are mentioned, ask **How would you feel if someone gave you that same advice about your children? How helpful would these suggestions be?**

## Step 2—Jacob's Road to Reconciliation (15 minutes)

Comment: We've considered one cause of conflict within a family. Obviously, there are many more reasons why family members get into conflicts, with one another. While there are things parents can do to head off conflicts, or at least reduce their severity, even the "best" of families will experience conflict. Let's move 20 years on in the story of Jacob to see six actions Jacob took to peacefully resolve his long-term dispute with Esau.

Divide the class into at least six groups of no more than four to six people per group. If you have fewer than 12 people, form three groups. Assign each group one or two of the references in Genesis 32 or 33. Give this instruction: **Read your verses and seek to identify what action Jacob took to help resolve his conflict with Esau.**

Allow three or four minutes for groups to read and talk. Show just the heading of the "Actions that Help Resolve Conflict" transparency. Explain that you have a list of Jacob's actions that may use different words to describe Jacob's efforts to resolve conflict. **First, I'd like to hear what you discovered, then I'll uncover that item on the transparency so that we can compare and see how you have improved on what I have.** Move in order through the groups, inviting a volunteer from each group to tell what he or she discovered about resolving conflict. As each group shares, uncover that point on the transparency:

1. Taking the initiative in communication (see Gen. 32:3-6);

2. Identifying the conflict or problem (see Gen. 32:11);

3. Praying about the problem (see Gen. 32:9);

4. Seeing the other person's perspective (see Gen. 32:20)—Comment that Jacob's gifts and repeated messages indicate at least a partial effort to think of Esau's needs and interests in this situation. He was thinking ahead, imagining Esau's response to his approach;

5. Telling how you feel (see Gen. 33:3,4)—Point out that Jacob's repeated bows very powerfully expressed his feelings of respect for Esau, something he had not shown when he defrauded his brother out of his birthright and blessing. Their mutual tears say more than any words about the true state of their feelings for each other;

6. Taking action to correct the problem:

• Make restitution (see Gen. 33:10,11)—Point out that Jacob's gifts were a tangible indication that he knew he had taken something of great value from his brother;

• Offer forgiveness and acceptance instead of seeking to get even or ahead (see Gen. 33:4,10,11).

## Option

This option will add five minutes to the Step 2 section.

Invite volunteers to tell of a conflict situation when one or more of Jacob's six actions was helpful in achieving a peaceful resolution. Be prepared to share an incident from your own family experiences to set a pattern for sharing. Be willing to show your own imperfections as well as your efforts to improve.

**Note:** If you are completing this session in one meeting, ignore this break and continue with Step 3.

**Two-Meeting Track:** If you want to spread this session over two meetings, **STOP** here and close in prayer. Inform group members of the content to be covered in your next meeting.

## Start Option (10 minutes)

Begin your second meeting by providing a blank sheet of paper and access to marking pens for each person. As they arrive, instruct them to draw large giftwrapped packages with tags addressed to family members with whom they have each had a recent conflict. On the outside of the package they are to letter boldly a "gift" they feel would help make peace with that family member—a contemporary version of Jacob's gift to Esau of goats, sheep, cows, camels and donkeys. The gift could be something tangible, an action, a message—anything that could convey a desire to reestablish harmony. Have ready a sample representing your own approach to resolving conflict with a family member.

Reserve three to five minutes for people to form groups of four or five members and briefly explain their gifts. Then continue with Step 3.

## Step 3—Teaching Forgiveness (10 minutes)

Show the three signs: "Forgive," "Excuse" and "Condone." Ask **What is the difference between these very similar words?** (*Condone* means to overlook an offense, thus tacitly allowing the action. *Excuse* means to forego punishment or restitution, but may convey the sense of keeping track of the misdeed—"I'll excuse you THIS time!" *Forgive* means to grant pardon without recalling the misdeed or being resentful for it.) Comment: **To say that I am willing to forgive, but I won't forget, means I haven't really forgiven. One of the reasons conflicts are so difficult to resolve is that truly forgiving someone who has offended us is not done easily.**

Ask **Why is it so often difficult for us to forgive someone we feel has offended us?** Accept ideas, then ask **What are some ways we can help our children learn to forgive each other and to forgive us?** (Forgiveness is most effectively learned through having been forgiven. Parents who want their children to learn to forgive must practice forgiveness toward the child, toward each other, and toward persons outside the family who may have offended the parent in some way. This includes a parent asking for the child's forgiveness when the parent has done something wrong.)

Ask **How can a parent decide when to forgive a child's misbehavior and when to impose unpleasant, but needed, consequences?** (The child's attitude is a key here. If the child is defiant, forgiveness is inappropriate. Without confession—an admission of being at fault—there is no basis on that to offer forgiveness. Also, children simply may not understand that they have done something wrong until they experience an unpleasant consequence for their misbehavior. In such cases, a parent may need to refrain from offering forgiveness until the consequences for the misbehavior have been imposed.)

After participants have shared ideas and experiences in response to this question, it will probably be obvious that often there is no clear indicator that assures a parent when to forgive and when to chastise. This is a good time to refer to the great promise of James 1:5: "If any of you lacks wisdom, he should ask God, who gives generously to all without finding fault."

### Option

This option will add 10 minutes to the Step 3 section.

At the top of the chalkboard or a blank overhead transparency, letter "GOAL: Restore Relationship." At the bottom, letter "OFFENDING BEHAVIOR." Draw an arrow from the bottom line pointing up to the top line. Across the center of that arrow, letter "CHANGE." Then, at the far left, letter "PUNISH?" and at the far right, letter "FORGIVE?"

Explain the diagram: **When a family member does something that offends us and our relationship is strained, our objective should be to find a way to restore that relationship. Somewhere along the line, in order for that process of restoration to be achieved, a change in behavior or attitude is necessary, usually in both**

parties. The offender needs to stop the hurtful behavior or attitude, and the one who is offended cannot harbor a grudge or a desire for revenge. Now, the question before us is, "Which of these two opposite approaches is most likely to achieve this desired result?" Lead the group in listing pros and cons for both punishing and forgiving as ways to restore a relationship. Ask **What does punishment accomplish that could help in restoration? How might punishment interfere with restoration?** Ask similar questions in considering forgiveness. Keep the group focused on the goal of restoration. As necessary, point out that we often lose sight of that goal when we have been offended, and emotions such as anger, jealousy and hurt feelings, cause us to react in ways that further damage the relationship, rather than restore it. When we respond to a family member in order to "get even" (Esau's reaction when he discovered that Jacob had defrauded him), we add to the problem, rather than help to resolve it.

Some people may feel that punishment is necessary in order to get a person to change his or her misbehavior. They tend to view punishment as a show of strength, while forgiveness is seen as a weaker response, somehow letting the offender "off the hook." On the contrary, having a new life in Christ is built on the power of forgiveness. The change from sinner to saint is accomplished in every believer's life, not through God's punishing acts, but through His love and mercy. Punishment is reserved for those who reject God's love. Those who accept it are transformed. As Christians, we need to learn to forgive, trusting God's power to change human behavior through forgiveness.

## Step 4 Option—Letting Go of a Grudge (15 minutes)

Comment: One of the most difficult things to do when we have been offended is to overcome feelings of resentment and anger toward the person who mistreated us. Jacob and Esau, even after their tearful reunion, perhaps found that the memories of their long animosity were hard to put aside. Read aloud Genesis 33:12-17.

Divide into groups of four or five people. Instruct each group to share ideas for not holding onto negative feelings about a family member's offending behavior. **What are some ways we can keep from letting frustrations and anger build in dealing with family problems? How do we keep from calling up past offenses in dealing with current situations?** Allow three to five minutes for groups to talk, then invite volunteers to share their group's best ideas.

Be prepared to suggest an idea or two of your own. A few helpful approaches include:
- pray for the other person's well-being (It's hard to pray for good things to happen to someone and stay mad at the same time.);
- pray for healing for your own feelings, asking God to replace your animosity with feelings of love and concern;
- make a list of all the positive things you respect in the other person as a reminder to yourself of the value of your relationship;

• ask the other person to forgive you for your attitude, being careful not to sling any accusations in the process;

• admit your resentments to a trusted friend, pastor or counselor (Talking about our feelings is a good way to control them.);

• if your anger is directed toward a child, ask your spouse to handle the next few discipline situations.

# Getting Personal
## (10 minutes)

Comment: **Learning to forgive is dependent on being forgiven. As parents, we are sometimes called upon to teach our children things we have not fully learned ourselves.** Distribute copies of "Oops! Pardon Me!" Instruct participants to write the names of their family members (may include those no longer living with them) on the figures drawn on the page. Below those figures, each participant is to list at least one action or attitude for that he or she needs that person's forgiveness, and/or one action or attitude for that he or she needs to forgive that person. Share one or two examples from your own completed page. Point out the bold "CONFIDENTIAL" stamp, that indicates that nothing on this page needs to be shared with anyone else.

Allow about five minutes for people to write. Then ask each person to circle one item on his or her sheet that he or she intends to act upon this week. **Select one person from whom you intend to ask for forgiveness, or whom you will forgive. Again, you will not be asked to share this choice with anyone else.**

### Getting Personal Option

This option will add 5-10 minutes to the Getting Personal section.

Instruct people to form groups of four or five people each. Within each group, starting with the person whose family moved the most during his or her childhood years, each person shares a one-sentence insight about forgiveness in family relationships. This could be an insight gained from this session or from a person's experiences in family living. Share an example or two of your own, i.e., "It's really hard for me to ask anyone in my family to forgive me when I've blown it—but it's always worth it."

Conclude the session by reading aloud Matthew 7:3-5 and Colossians 3:13. Then close in prayer.

Announce that the next session will focus on commitment to family members.

# ACTIONS THAT Help Resolve Conflict

1. Take the initiative in communication (see Genesis 32:3-6);

2. Identify the conflict or problem (see Genesis 32:11);

3. Pray about the problem (see Genesis 32:9);

4. See the other person's perspective (see Genesis 32:20);

5. Tell how you feel (see Genesis 33:3,4);

6. Take action to correct the problem:

 • Make restitution (see Genesis 33:10,11);
 • Offer forgiveness and acceptance instead of seeking to get even or ahead (see Genesis 33:4,10,11).

"Bear with each other and forgive whatever grievances you may have against one another. Forgive as the Lord forgave you" (Colossians 3:13).

# "Oops! Pardon Me!"

Write the names of your family members (may include those no longer living with you) on some or all of these figures. Below each figure, list at least one action or attitude for which you need that person's forgiveness, and/or one action or attitude for which you need to forgive that person.

**Note:** This activity is to help you think of forgiveness in specific situations. Nothing written on this page needs to be shared with anyone.

"Why do you look at the speck of sawdust in your brother's eye and pay no attention to the plank in your own eye? How can you say to your brother, 'Let me take the speck out of your eye,' when all the time there is a plank in your own eye? You hypocrite, first take the plank out of your own eye, and then you will see clearly to remove the speck from your brother's eye" (Matthew 7:3-5).

# Commitment: Ruth and Naomi Are Faithful

## Session Keys

### Key Verses

"Let love and faithfulness never leave you; bind them about your neck, write them on the tablet of your heart. Then you will win favor and a good name in the sight of God and man." Proverbs 3:3,4

"Be devoted to one another in brotherly love. Honor one another above yourselves." Romans 12:10

### Key Idea

Successful families follow the Lord's direction to be faithful and committed to each other.

### Key Readings

Ruth 1; 2:2,17-19

## Preparation

We live in an age when it seems difficult for anyone to make commitments, let alone keep them once they are made.

1. National leaders seem to haggle endlessly over treaties, that are soon discarded.
2. Professional athletes seek to renegotiate contracts they recently approved.
3. Couples experiment with living together without getting married, and vast numbers of marriages end in divorce.
4. Children who have been raised by a succession of day care providers grow to adolescence without bonding to any adult.
5. Even church members are reluctant to accept responsibility in essential areas of ministry.

The story of Ruth and Naomi can help us learn the value of making and keeping commitments in our families. We can discover the benefits of following through on our agreements. A sense of security and belonging grows only when family members can truly depend on each other, especially when circumstances are difficult.

But what of your commitment to the people you are teaching? Does your responsibility to them end when you dismiss them from this session? When the course is over?

The weeks and months that follow this course are fertile opportunities to extend the impact of these few sessions. How might you express an ongoing commitment to the people you are now teaching? A few ideas:

1. Pray for them regularly—by name;
2. Send an encouraging card or letter;

3. Invite them to attend a church activity (or some other event) with you;

4. Plan a class "reunion" a few weeks after the course concludes, with an opportunity for people to share experiences related to the topics discussed;

5. Seek out participants when opportunities arise (before or after church services, in the parking lot, etc.), showing continued interest in their families;

6. Explore ways to befriend a specific family with an evident need for support.

Provide blank name tags and felt-tip pens. Wear a tag yourself.

Provide these materials:

Choice 1: Cut bumper-sticker-sized strips of colored paper, one per person. Have ready felt-tip markers, one per four to six people, and masking tape. On two larger sheets of paper, letter "Promises My Kids Always Remember" on one and "Promises My Kids Tend to Forget" on the other. Mount these on opposite walls. Place masking tape loops (sticky side out) on the walls beneath each sheet, one loop per person.

Make a transparency of "Some Questions About Commitment" on page 55.

Cut blank paper into pocket-sized pieces, one piece per person. Have ready pencils or pens for those who may need them.

Duplicate on bright-colored paper copies of "Sticking It Out" on page 57.

Getting Started Option: Letter the words of Proverbs 3:3,4 on large index cards, one or two words per card. Separate the card with the word "Then" as well as the three cards that immediately precede and the three that immediately follow that card. Mix up the remaining cards. Have ready some chocolate kisses to give to the winning team(s).

Have ready a chalkboard and chalk and/or an overhead projector with blank transparencies and transparency pens.

Letter two large signs: "Bethlehem" and "Moab." Mount them on opposite walls. Letter seven smaller signs, six with the names of the characters in the first chapter of Ruth: Naomi, Elimelech, Mahlon, Kilion, Orpah, Ruth; the seventh says "10 Years."

Letter Ruth 1:16,17 on a poster or blank transparency, drawing a single blank line in place of the name "Ruth" and any first person pronouns (me, I, my). Draw a double blank line in place of the second person pronouns (you, your).

# Session 3 at a Glance

| SECTION | ONE-SESSION PLAN | | TWO-SESSION PLAN | WHAT YOU'LL DO |
|---|---|---|---|---|
| | 60 to 75 Minutes | More than 75 Minutes | 60 Minutes (each session) | |
| Getting Started | 10 | 10-20 | *Session One:* 20 | Introduce Keeping Promises |
| Getting into the Word | 40 | 60-75 | 40 | Consider an Example of Commitment |
| Step 1 | 10 | 15 | 15 | When the Going Gets Tough... |
| Step 2 | 20 | 25 | 25 | Ruth's Decision and Determination |
| | | | *Session Two Start Option:* 10 | People Today... Agree/Disagree |
| Step 3 | 10 | 20 | 20 | Sticking It Out |
| (Step 4 Option) | (15) | (15) | 15 | When Commitments Are Broken |
| Getting Personal | 10 | 10-15 | 15 | Making a Promise |

# Session Plan

## Leader's Choice

**Two-Meeting Track:** This session is designed to be completed in one 60- to 75-minute meeting. If you want to extend the session over two meetings and allow group members more time for discussion, **END** your first meeting and **BEGIN** your second meeting at the stop-and-go symbol in the session plan.

The boxes marked with the clock symbol provide optional learning experiences to extend this session over two meetings or to accommodate a session longer than 60-75 minutes.

# Getting Started

## (10 minutes)

## Choice 1—Promises, Promises

Welcome people as they arrive and guide them to make (or find) and wear a name tag. To help people continue to get acquainted and build relationships, have people form groups of up to six people each. Give each group four strips of colored paper and a marking pen. Call attention to the two sheets of paper mounted on opposite walls, "Promises My Kids Always Remember" and "Promises My Kids Tend to Forget." Share an example or two from your own family (i.e., "My kids always remember that I promised to take them to Disney World someday. But they have a hard time remembering their numerous promises to stop bugging each other."). Instruct the groups to share with each other some specific examples of both types of promises, then select two of each and letter them on the paper strips provided. When they finish their four strips, they are to take them to the appropriate side of the room and use the masking tape loops to attach them to the wall.

When most groups have completed the assignment, read aloud several of the promises on each wall. Then ask **What does this display of promises tell us about our children?** Accept several responses, that will probably point out the natural tendency to "selectively" remember: recall the things they like and forget what they don't like. Then ask, **As mature, responsible adults, how different are we in remembering and keeping promises?** Most people will conclude that adults share that same tendency to selectively remember.

Transition into today's topic: **In this session we will explore the issue of commitment in our families—the realization that making and keeping promises is essential to the health and stability of every family relationship.**

## Choice 2—One-Minute Stories

Welcome people as they arrive and guide them to make (or find) and wear name tags. To help people begin to get acquainted and build relationships, have them form groups of four or five people. Introduce this activity: **Everybody likes a good story and everybody has a wealth of good stories from his or her own life experiences. Each group member is going to tell a one-minute story about a promise. Think of an incident involving you and someone close to you—a family member, a relative, a friend—when a promise was made and either broken or kept. Your story can be from any period of your life, your childhood, your teen years or your adulthood. As you tell your story, try to keep your audience in a little bit of suspense about the outcome, and make sure you tell how that outcome, the promise either being kept or broken, affected your relationship with that person.**

To establish a pattern (and to give people a few moments to think), tell a story from your own experiences. Be sure you keep it within the one-minute limit. Then have each group select a timekeeper to alert each storyteller when their minute is up. Suggest that the first storyteller should be the person in the group who most recently did the family laundry.

When groups finish telling their stories, ask **From thinking about your own experiences and listening to the stories of others, how is a relationship affected when promises are kept? When a promise is broken?** Allow several people to respond.

Transition into the session topic by commenting: **Everyone has unintentionally or intentionally broken promises. In this session we will explore the issue of commitment in our families, and that making and keeping promises is essential to the health and stability of every family relationship.**

## Getting Started Option: Powerful Proverb Game

This option will add 10 minutes to the Getting Started section.

Keep the participants in the same small groups. Evenly distribute the index cards with the words from Proverbs 3:3,4 among the small groups, retaining the card with the word "Then" plus any other words that immediately precede or follow "Then" so that all groups have the same number of cards. (Example: If you made 25 cards and there are five groups, give each group four cards and retain the middle five. If you have six groups, give each group four cards and just retain "Then".) Introduce the activity: **The cards I just distributed contain the words of two verses from the book of Proverbs. The first verse gives a very important instruction to us, and the second verse conveys a great promise if we carry out that instruction.** Hold up the card(s) you retained. **The word "then" is the beginning of the promise. Your group's assignment is to earn points as we work together to put this proverb in order, working backwards and forwards from this key word. Your group will earn 10 points if you bring up a word that immediately precedes or follows whatever words have been added. However, if you bring up an incorrect word, your team loses one point.**

Call on each "team" in turn to bring up a word and place it at the front or end of the word(s) displayed. A team may pass one time during the game if it feels none of its cards can be used at present. When a word "fits," have that team member stay up front and hold that card. (If you have more cards than people, mount the cards to a bulletin board or wall as they are added to the verse.)

Mark each team's score on the chalkboard or an overhead transparency.

When the verse is completed, give chocolate kisses to the winning team members, then lead the group in reading the proverb aloud in unison. Ask **What does this proverb say to us about the issue of commitment in family living?** Allow several people to comment.

# Getting into the Word

## (40 minutes)

### Step 1—When the Going Gets Tough... (10 minutes)

Comment: Many people feel that our society does not place a high value on fulfilling commitments. For example, we commonly joke about campaign promises made by politicians, as though no one really expects elected officials to actually do what they said in their quests for election. Ask the group to suggest other examples of broken promises and commitments from their observations of contemporary life. Be prepared to share a few if needed to encourage participation (divorce, advertising that promises more than the product delivers, etc.).

After a variety of responses, invite the group to focus on commitments within the family. Ask **What are some of the commitments that family members make to each other?** As ideas are shared, it should quickly become obvious that some family commitments involve matters of great import and span a wide range of activities and years (i.e., marriage itself; parental commitments to feed, clothe, instruct children; etc.), while other commitments are relatively minor and short-term (i.e, a promise to do something at a certain time). However, all commitments made within a family impact each person's sense of trust and well-being.

Lead the group in suggesting reasons why family commitments are broken. Ask **Why do we let each other down by not following through on what we have promised?** As group members suggest reasons, list them on the chalkboard or on an overhead transparency as either internal and/or external factors. Internal factors are the many human imperfections and weaknesses. External factors are the circumstances of our lives that apply pressure, often resulting in our inner weaknesses betraying our good intentions.

### Option

This option will add five minutes to the Step 1 section.

Refer to the list of reasons people have suggested for why family members sometimes fail in their commitments to each other. Comment: **With all these reasons for why family commitments are broken, it would seem unlikely that any commitments are ever kept.** Ask What makes the difference between the times we succeed in following through with our commitments and the times we do not? Add these ideas to another column on the chalkboard or transparency. Avoid evaluating or commenting on the ideas at this time.

### Step 2—Ruth's Decision and Determination (20 minutes)

Ask for volunteers to represent the main characters in Ruth 1: Naomi, Elimelech, Mahlon, Kilion, Orpah and Ruth. Give each one a name sign and point out the

Bethlehem and Moab signs on opposite sides of the room. Instruct the "actors" to move as the narrative indicates. Encourage them to use a little creative imagination in expressing the emotions described in the story. Then read aloud chapter 1 of Ruth, pausing as necessary to allow the characters to enact the scenes as you read the verses:

1,2—Elimelech, Naomi and their two sons start out by the Bethlehem sign, then move to the Moab sign.

3—Elimelech dies, so the family is probably sad.

4—Orpah and Ruth join Mahlon and Kilion; the newlyweds look happy; Naomi probably looks suspicious. Hold up "10 Years" sign.

5—Mahlon and Kilion die; the women grieve.

6,7—The women start toward Bethlehem.

8-13—Naomi tries to send Orpah and Ruth home; they all weep.

14-18—Orpah returns to Moab; Ruth clings to Naomi.

19-22—Naomi and Ruth return to Bethlehem.

After thanking the "actors," comment, **This story of a mother-in-law and daughter-in-law is one of the greatest illustrations of commitment within a family. What did Naomi and Ruth do to show the depth of their commitment to each other?** (Naomi sought what she felt was Ruth and Orpah's best opportunity by encouraging them to return home to Moab. Their tears showed not only their sadness for their own losses, but their caring for each other. Ruth's declaration is a classic statement of lifelong commitment to a family member.)

Ask **How realistic was Ruth's declaration? Was she burdening herself with more responsibility than a person should reasonably be expected to perform?** Allow group members to share their perspectives, then ask, **Based on the little bit we know about these women from this chapter, what do you imagine might have happened during the previous 10 years** (hold up sign again) **to lead Ruth to make such a declaration?** Again, allow people to express their ideas. Point out that, while the Bible gives us no details about those 10 years, it is more than reasonable to assume that a strong relationship of love and trust had developed between Naomi and Ruth. Ruth's declaration was most likely a verbal expression of an ongoing pattern of mutual caring for one another.

Uncover the top of "Some Questions About Commitment" transparency. Guide a discussion of Ruth's commitment to Naomi by asking the questions on the transparency:

**What are some likely reasons Ruth could have given for leaving Naomi to continue on her own?**

**Is commitment of the degree Ruth promised necessary in family relationships? Is it possible in today's society?**

**What happens to family members when this kind of commitment is not present?**

**What is the impact on family relationships when family members share a high level of commitment to each other?**

What has to exist in a relationship for family members to make such a commitment?

As people share their thoughts, be prepared, if needed, to point out that a strong mutual commitment among family members is essential both to the health and stability of the family and for the individuals within it. One of a child's deepest and most basic needs is for a sense of security, that only grows as a child learns that parents can be counted on when needed. The familiar toddler trauma of separation anxiety when parents leave the child is powerful evidence of the child's dependence on parents. Learning to trust that Mom and Dad will come back is a major milestone in a child's development. As children grow older, the need for dependable family relationships becomes less obvious, but no less real. Children who have been abused or neglected are severely hampered in developing the ability to trust and love another person. Even as adults, that need for commitment remains a powerful part of all our lives.

Conclude this discussion by pointing out that the remaining chapters of the book of Ruth recount that Ruth's declaration was not mere words, but was followed by a pattern of actions that carried out her statement. Not only did Ruth's evident loyalty to Naomi play a vital role in impressing Boaz to seek to marry Ruth, the "icing on the cake" is outlined in the final two verses in that we discover that the great-grandson of Ruth and Boaz was David. A woman of Moab, a people who had harassed Israel since the days of Moses, became an honored member of the lineage of David, and ultimately of the Messiah. She is mentioned again in Matthew 1:5, a lasting example of the power in making and keeping commitments in the face of difficulties.

## Option

This option will add five minutes to the Step 2 section.

Give each person a blank pocket-sized piece of paper. Provide pencils or pens to those who need them. Read aloud Ruth 2:11, Boaz's explanation to Ruth of why he was being generous towards her. Then give the following instructions: **Imagine you were meeting someone who knew about you and your family. Write down what he or she might say was common knowledge about your commitment to the people in your family. Would this stranger say, "Frankly, with you being gone from home so much, and leaving your family on their own so often, I wonder if you're really in it for the long haul"? Or, could you honestly write, "I've been told all about what you have done for your wife and children, how you plan your schedule to spend as much time with them as possible, how you consider them first in decisions you make, etc."?** Assure people they will not be asked to share this statement with anyone. It's a small piece of paper you can keep tucked in your wallet or pocket to encourage you to demonstrate a higher degree of commitment to your family members.

**Note:** If you are completing this session in one meeting, ignore this break and continue with Step 3.

**Two-Meeting Track:** If you want to spread this session over two meetings, STOP here and close in prayer. Inform group members of the content to be covered in your next meeting.

## Start Option (10 minutes)

Begin your second meeting by lettering this statement on the chalkboard or on an overhead transparency: "People today don't have commitments—we have useful relationships and meaningful encounters."

As people arrive, invite them to ask at least three other people whether they tend to agree or disagree with the statement.

After several minutes, ask for a show of hands of those who agree and those who disagree with the statement. If there are people on both sides of the issue, instruct people to sit on the left side of the room if they tend to agree with the statement, or on the right side of the room if they tend to disagree with it. If most people are all on one side of the issue, simply invite people to be seated.

Ask a volunteer to tell one reason why he or she agrees or disagrees with the statement. If there are those who take the other position, ask someone on the other side to give one reason to support his or her opinion. Or ask for anyone to tell a reason someone might give for supporting that position. Continue alternating between the two points of view in soliciting people's reactions to the statement. (You might encourage people to move to the other side of the room if they hear a reason that convinces them to change their mind. This procedure helps people consider information with an open mind.)

After people have had an opportunity to express their ideas, offer this comment: **There obviously is a difference between commitment and "useful relationships" or "meaningful encounters." Whether or not we perceive ourselves or our society as lacking in commitment, we do know that when the going gets tough, a lot of people bail out. In this session, we're going to explore factors that can help us maintain our commitments to one another, and teach our children to do the same, in the face of difficulties, not just when it's convenient.** Then continue with Step 3 and conclude the session.

## Step 3—Sticking It Out (10 minutes)

Distribute copies of "Sticking It Out." Then divide the class into groups of four or five people. Instruct half of the groups to compile ideas that can help us in keeping our promises to our family. The other half will compile ideas for teaching our kids to do the same. Call attention to the two "starter" ideas in each column. Allow three or four minutes for groups to write down as many ideas as they can.

Allow an additional minute for groups to select their best idea, writing it near the bottom of the page. Then invite a volunteer from each group to share that idea with the rest of the class. As ideas are shared, help to clarify the ideas whenever necessary.

Ask questions such as those suggested on the page: **How would doing that help me to follow through on my commitment to my wife? When might be a time I could actually do that? Could you give us an example of how a parent of a (toddler/preschooler/teenager) could do that?**

## Option

This option will add 10 minutes to the Step 3 section.

Point out that while the customs described in Ruth are very different from ours, we see clearly displayed in chapters 3 and 4 a high degree of integrity and compassion in the fulfillment of family commitments. Instruct half of the groups to read Ruth 3:1-11, while the other half reads Ruth 4:1-10. Group members are to identify from their narrative any insights regarding making and following through on commitments. Allow five or six minutes for groups to read and talk, then invite volunteers to share their insights. Among the things people are likely to note:

Naomi was concerned about Ruth's future, even at the risk of Ruth's attention and affection being drawn away from Naomi (see 3:1).

Naomi obviously gave careful thought to a plan that could benefit Ruth (see 3:2-4).

Ruth clearly trusted Naomi's intentions and judgment (see 3:5,6).

Ruth was careful in her approach to Boaz to avoid any hint of public pressure, while clearly stating her desire (see 3:7-9). The request to "spread the corner of your garment over me" was clearly intended and understood to be asking Boaz to become her protector, her husband.

Boaz was gentle and understanding, seeking to handle this delicate situation in the best possible manner for her benefit (see 3:10,11).

Boaz, who was evidently considerably older than Ruth, was considerate of the feelings of Naomi's closest relative, and thus of Naomi, also (see 4:1-4). A "kinsman-redeemer" was the nearest male relative who could rightfully marry a widow and pass on her family's heritage and property to their children.

Boaz had clearly thought through all the implications of the situation and was very clear in explaining the full circumstances to the relative, thus avoiding a hasty, and possibly unhappy, decision (see 4:5,6).

The curious custom of exchanging a sandal is an example of the value of symbolic gestures in defining and expressing commitments in a relationship (see 4:7,8).

Boaz made his commitment public, gaining the support of his community (see 4:2,9,10).

## Step 4 Option—When Commitments Are Broken (15 minutes)

Comment: Most people tend to make a distinction between major commitments, such as the one Ruth made to Naomi or a couple makes when they get married, and the relatively minor commitments of everyday life. Forgetting to stop by the store on the way home, backing out of a social obligation at the last minute, beg-

ging off a promise to play catch with a child seem unimportant compared to larger, lifelong promises. However, all promises we keep or break impact the level of trust between people, significantly affecting the quality of the relationship. Especially in guiding the development of children, the small promises of life make a big difference in a child becoming a person who can be counted on in life's bigger issues.

Lead the class in discussing the problem of how to act when a promise is not kept. Raise the following issues, inviting suggestions from group members on ways to restore trust and strengthen relationships:

• When we are the one who forgot, or ignored, or intentionally broke a promise, what are some "less than helpful" actions we tend to try? (Be prepared to share an example or two of your own. Most commonly, people tend to try to avoid responsibility by making excuses, blaming others or attempting to justify their actions: "Why didn't you remind me?" or "I was so busy it just slipped my mind.") Why are those actions not helpful in restoring trust? What are some more helpful ways we could respond?

• When a child has reneged on a promise, what actions can we take to help the child become more dependable in the future? Note: Recall the previous session on forgiveness. Ask, **Won't letting a child 'off the hook' simply make it easy for him or her to repeat the offense?** (Remind the class that forgiveness is not simply ignoring the problem. Forgiveness is cancelling a debt that has been acknowledged by both parties.)

• When a spouse has broken a promise, how can we help to restore trust to the relationship? (Accusations and name-calling may let off steam, but they tend to further divide, rather than heal. A clear statement of how a person feels about a breach of promise can help the other party to recognize the implications of his or her actions, that is an important step toward restoration. However, when a person places his or her desires ahead of the other person's well-being, a deep chasm will remain. When a relationship is built on "What can I get out of it?"—trouble looms ahead.) Emphasize that someone living with a person who repeatedly breaks promises does not need to live as a victim. Repeated promises to "never do it again" do not have to be blindly accepted. Instead, ask the person, "What could I do to help you keep that promise?" "How can we work together to rebuild trust and love in our relationship?" Praying together, asking God's best for the other person, is a powerful means of enabling healing to occur.

# Getting Personal
## (10 minutes)

Show the poster or transparency of Ruth 1:16,17. Read the two verses aloud, inserting your name in each single blank line, and the name of a family member in each double blank line. Then invite everyone to read the verses silently, inserting their own name in each single blank line and the name of a family member in each double blank line. Repeat once or twice, suggesting that people select a different family member's name to insert, or choose the same one again.

After the readings, ask people to form pairs. Married couples can be together, and those who do not have a spouse present can find another unattached person. Each person then tells his or her partner, "In order to keep a promise like that, I need to...." Each person should tell at least two specific decisions or actions that would help in keeping such a promise.

## Getting Personal Option

This option will add 5-10 minutes to the Getting Personal section.

Have people retain the same partners, this time asking each other, "What could I do to help you keep your commitments to your family?" Depending on how well partners know each other, suggest that they may ask each other for prayer, for an occasional reminder or word of encouragement, or even for some practical assistance.

Conclude the session by closing in prayer.

Announce that the next session will focus on communication with family members.

# Some Questions About Commitment

What are some likely reasons Ruth could have given for leaving Naomi to continue on her own?

........................................................................................................................

........................................................................................................................

Is commitment of the degree Ruth promised necessary in family relationships?

........................................................................................................................

........................................................................................................................

Is it possible in today's society?

........................................................................................................................

........................................................................................................................

What happens to family members when this kind of commitment is not present?

........................................................................................................................

........................................................................................................................

What is the impact on family relationships when family members share a high level of commitment to each other?

........................................................................................................................

........................................................................................................................

What has to exist in a relationship for family members to make such a commitment?

........................................................................................................................

........................................................................................................................

........................................................................................................................

# Sticking It Out

Keeping Our Promises
- Write it down.
- Tell the other person.

Teaching Our Children
- Set a positive example.
- Affirm their successes.

The Best Idea:
.................................................................

How would doing that help me to follow through on my commitment to my (spouse/child)?
.................................................................

When might be a time I could actually do that?
.................................................................

How could a parent of a (toddler/preschooler/teenager) do that?
.................................................................
.................................................................

# Communication: David and Jonathan Show Love

## Session Keys

### Key Verses

"From the fruit of his lips a man is filled with good things as surely as the work of his hands rewards him." Proverbs 12:14

"Everyone should be quick to listen, slow to speak and slow to become angry." James 1:19

### Key Idea

Successful families follow the Lord's direction to communicate effectively with each other, openly expressing love and affection.

### Key Readings

1 Samuel 17:48-58; 18:1—19:12; 20:1-42; 23:15-18

## Preparation

David and Jonathan provided friendship and support for one another when their biological families were not able to do so. Jonathan's father was tormented by an evil spirit and had become dangerously depressed, attacking even his own son. While not estranged from his family, David had left his home to enter the service of King Saul.

We are impressed with the strength of friendship between the two young brothers-in-law—a friendship that flourished under stress that would have shattered many relationships. We observe a dramatic contrast in the way King Saul dealt with pressures and how David and Jonathan responded.

Saul:

1. sought to manipulate others to resolve problems (see 1 Sam. 18:15-21);

2. lashed out in anger, blaming others (see 1 Sam. 20:30-33).

David and Jonathan:

1. affirmed (spoke well of) each other (see 1 Sam. 19:4);

2. spoke lovingly and honestly to each other (see 1 Sam. 19:7);

3. showed restraint by not retaliating to hurt someone, even when attacked or angry (see 1 Sam. 19:10; 20:34);

4. listened to what the other one said (see 1 Sam. 20);

5. expressed their feelings (see 1 Sam. 20:41);

6. encouraged each other (see 1 Sam. 23:15-18).

Effective communication is vital in any relationship, especially within a family. Most people need help in learning effective communication skills, particularly when dealing with strong emotions. Family members who do not know how to express feelings are likely to either withdraw into a shell or go to the other extreme and lash out violently. In contrast, families who establish patterns of open communication build strong bonds of understanding and affection. Parental examples of listening to each other and encouraging children when they speak are valuable aids in helping both parent and child grow in this important area of life.

Provide blank name tags and felt-tip pens. Wear a tag yourself.

Provide these materials:

Choice 1: A large map of the world, mounted on a bulletin board or wall; three different colors of paper cut into tags about one-half-inch high and two-inches wide (one tag per person of one color, two tags per person of the second color, four tags per person of the third color); fine-tip pens; and straight pins or masking tape.

Choice 2: Make six signs, each lettered with one word or phrase: "Pay Attention," "Good Job," "You're in Trouble," "Supper Time," "I Love You" and "Stop It." Mount the signs on walls around the room.

Duplicate on bright-colored paper copies of "Communication Barriers" on page 69, making one per person.

On eight large index cards, letter the following assignments (If you will have more than eight groups of four or five people each, make additional duplicate cards):

1. Manipulate (see 1 Samuel 18:15-21)
2. Blame (see 1 Samuel 20:30-33)
3. Affirm (see 1 Samuel 19:4-6)
4. Loving Honesty (see 1 Samuel 19:1-3,7; 20:12-17)
5. Restraint (see 1 Samuel 18:10,11; 19:10; 20:30-34)
6. Listen (see 1 Samuel 20:1-4)
7. Express Feelings (see 1 Samuel 20:41,42)
8. Encourage (see 1 Samuel 23:15-18)

Make a transparency of "Saying What I Feel" on page 71.

# Session 4 at a Glance

| SECTION | ONE-SESSION PLAN | | TWO-SESSION PLAN | WHAT YOU'LL DO |
|---|---|---|---|---|
| | 60 to 75 Minutes | More than 75 Minutes | 60 Minutes (each session) | |
| Getting Started | 10 | 10-20 | Session One: 20 | Introduce Family Communication |
| Getting into the Word | 40 | 60-75 | 40 | Contrasting Healthy and Unhealthy Communication |
| Step 1 | 10 | 15 | 15 | Communication Barriers |
| Step 2 | 20 | 25 | 25 | David, Jonathan and Saul |
| | | | Session Two Start Option: 10 | Oldest, Youngest, Middle, Only |
| Step 3 | 10 | 20 | 20 | Saying What I Feel |
| (Step 4 Option) | (15) | (15) | 15 | Nonverbal Communication Skills |
| Getting Personal | 10 | 10-15 | 15 | A Reason to Improve |

# Session Plan

### Leader's Choice

**Two-Meeting Track:** This session is designed to be completed in one 60- to 75-minute meeting. If you want to extend the session over two meetings and allow group members more time for discussion, **END** your first meeting and **BEGIN** your second meeting at the stop-and-go symbol in the session plan.

The boxes marked with the clock symbol provide optional learning experiences to extend this session over two meetings or to accommodate a session longer than 60-75 minutes.

# Getting Started

## (10 minutes)

### Choice 1—It's a Long, Long Way

Welcome people as they arrive and guide them to make (or find) and wear name tags. To help people continue to get acquainted and build relationships, have people note on the map of the world the places where they, their parents and their grandparents were born. Each person writes his or her name on the first colored tag and attaches it to the map to show his or her birthplace. People then write their parents' names on the second colored tags and attach them to the map. Finally, they write their grandparents' names on the third colored tags and attach them to the map. As people work on this project, encourage conversation about family migrations ("When did your family move here?"), about locations shared in common by some people ("Who would have thought that Shirley, Kim and Tony all came from the same place?"), and about locations that are unique within your group ("Didn't anyone else come from New Jersey?").

Once the map is suitably decorated, invite comments about some of the varied locales that were marked: **What does a map like this make you think about your own family? What would your children say if you showed them your tags on here? If we added our great-grandparents to the map, what other places would you be placing tags?**

Lead into today's study with these comments: **I heard of a child who was born in New York. His brother had been born in California. His two sisters had been born in Ontario, Canada and Oregon. His mother had been born in Minnesota and his father in England. When he thought about those widely separated birthplaces, he commented, "I wonder how we all met?"** While great physical distances separate some of us from the places where our families used to live, today we are going to explore some ways to bridge the emotional distances that can grow up between people who share the same house. We're going to investigate communication within the family.

### Choice 2—No Hidden Messages Here

Welcome people as they arrive and guide them to make (or find) and wear name tags. To help people continue to get acquainted and build relationships, call attention to the six message signs displayed around the room. Explain: **These are some common messages that parents give to children. We're going to start out this session by recalling some of the ways our own parents communicated these messages with us when we were young.** Share one or two examples from your own childhood: **When my dad wanted my attention, he'd snap his fingers. I always thought he had the loudest finger snap west of the Mississippi.**

Instruct people to join with at least one other person near a sign containing a message they remember their parents having communicated with them. Each person then shares how his or her parents delivered that message. (If your group members have become comfortable sharing with one another, suggest they demonstrate how the message was communicated.)

After a minute or two, instruct people to move to a different sign, gathering with at least some people who were not in their first group. Repeat this so people get to visit three or four of the signs, then instruct everyone to be seated.

Ask **Why do you think certain messages from our parents are still vividly remembered today?** (They were repeated often, they were loud or dramatic, we've used them with our own children, etc.) Then introduce today's topic: **While certain messages come through loud and clear, others are more difficult to get across. And sometimes the more difficult ones are the most important ones. Today we are going to explore the issue of effective family communication.**

### Getting Started Option: I Said, I Meant

This option will add 10 minutes to the Getting Started section.

Have participants form groups of four or five people each. Share an incident from your experiences when something you or another family member had said was misunderstood by another member of the family. ("I said, 'I'll pick you up after school.' I meant, 'I'll pick you up by the overpass.'") Then describe the problems that resulted from the misunderstanding. ("I waited by the overpass and he waited by the parking lot, and by the time we found each other, we were 20 minutes late for our meeting.")

Instruct group members to tell a similar incident from their experiences when the intended message was not fully understood by the other person, resulting in confusion or some other problem. In each group, the first person to share is the one who most recently took out the family trash.

After people have had time to share their stories, ask **How common is the problem of not fully communicating to another person what is perfectly clear to us?** (Obviously, this is a problem in all areas of life.) Then comment: **Seeing that we all have trouble at times getting someone else to understand what we mean, it is imperative that we explore the issue of effective communication in families.**

## Getting into the Word

### (40 minutes)

### Step 1—Communication Barriers (10 minutes)

With people in groups of four or five members, distribute copies of "Communication Barriers." Explain: **This page shows a family of isolated people. They are all in the same house, but they are cut off from communication with each other. As you** think about your own family and other families you know, what are some of the factors that get in the way of family members effectively communicating with each other? Talk about this question in your group, and write down, inside the rooms of the house on this worksheet, the barriers to communication your group members suggest. Encourage people to think of actions, attitudes and circumstances that inhibit good family interaction.

Allow four or five minutes for groups to talk and write. Then invite volunteers to each share one of the barriers their group discussed. As barriers to communication are mentioned, ask questions to help people think further about these difficulties: **How common is that problem? Why does that get in the way of good communication? What impact does that have on the relationships within a family?**

## Option

This option will add five minutes to the Step 1 section.

Read aloud James 1:19, explaining that it contains some very famous instructions about communication: **Everyone should be quick to listen, slow to speak and slow to become angry.** Ask **How would following this instruction aid in overcoming any of the barriers we've just talked about?** If necessary, refer to one or more specific barriers people had mentioned, and repeat the question: **How would following this instruction aid in overcoming the barrier of** (busy schedules, too much TV, self-centeredness, etc.)?

## Step 2—David, Jonathan and Saul (20 minutes)

Introduce the story of David and Jonathan as one of the most remarkable accounts of friendship and positive personal communication, especially in contrast with the very negative relationships involving King Saul. Briefly tell the story of David and Jonathan's friendship and family connections, giving just enough background to help people in completing the study assignments below. Among the points to bring out in telling the story:

• David and Jonathan became instant friends after David's victory over Goliath, while Saul quickly became jealous of David's popularity and began a campaign to remove David (see 1 Sam. 18:1-19). It is not evident whether Saul knew at this point that David had already been anointed by Samuel to become king (see 16:13), but Saul did know that God had rejected him as king (see 15:26) and would be likely to view an able warrior as a very real threat.

• Saul's daughter, Michal, fell in love with David. Saul sought to manipulate this situation to his advantage and David's destruction, but David triumphed and was married to Michal, becoming Jonathan's brother-in-law (see 1 Sam. 18:20-30).

• Jonathan sought to intervene with Saul on David's behalf, but Saul's animosity actually increased (see 1 Sam. 19:1-12).

• David sought out Jonathan and they talked together, promising to help each other and seeking a way to resolve the threat to David's life (see 1 Sam. 20). Seeing Jonathan's continuing ties to David infuriated Saul, causing him to voice for the first time his deep awareness that David was destined to assume the throne.

• Later, while David was living as a fugitive from Saul's army, Jonathan came to see him and encouraged him. This was evidently the last time they saw each other, and we see the remarkable lack of self-centeredness in the king's son declaring his willingness to serve under David's rule (see 1 Sam. 23:15-18).

• Throughout this story, we are repeatedly told of the strong bond of love between David and Jonathan (see 1 Sam. 18:1-4; 19:1; 20:17).

After completing this overview of David and Jonathan's friendship, divide the class into groups of four or five members. Give each group one of the assignment cards you prepared. If you have fewer than eight groups, give each group two cards. If you still have cards left, be prepared to share your own insights about the assignments you did not give out. If you have more than eight groups, some groups will have identical assignments.

Instruct the groups to read the verses and then discuss what they learn there (negatively or positively) about effective, positive communication in a relationship. Point out that the first two assignments look at Saul's destructive communication. The other six look at positive ways in which David and Jonathan communicated, resulting in their relationship being strengthened in spite of the pressures of Saul's animosity and the issue of succession to the throne. Allow four or five minutes for groups to read and talk.

Ask first for volunteers to share insights they gained about negative communication (assignments 1 and 2). Then ask for insights about positive communication. As people share, ask questions such as **How did that impact the relationship between David and Jonathan? Why is that a positive factor in good communication? When a relationship is under a lot of pressure, how does that help?**

Summarize this sharing of insights: **None of the positive communication skills are a remedy that guarantee smooth sailing in a relationship. We see clearly in chapter 20, in the questions that David and Jonathan ask each other, that some doubts have crept in. They are obviously wondering if they can still really trust each other. But they kept talking, and listening, and declaring their commitment to each other. And the communication patterns they used are still helpful in building bridges over the barriers that tend to separate us from one another.**

## Option

This option will add five minutes to the Step 2 section.

Read aloud Proverbs 12:14, "From the fruit of his lips a man is filled with good things as surely as the work of his hands rewards him." Comment: We usually think that saying positive things to someone is a benefit to the person we are addressing. This proverb shows us that positive communication brings good things to us. Ask **What are some of the benefits we gain from emphasizing positive communication with our family members? What benefits did David and Jonathan gain from their patterns of interaction? How would the story have been different if David or Jonathan had fallen into Saul's pattern of manipulating and blaming?**

**Note:** If you are completing this session in one meeting, ignore this break and continue with Step 3.

**Two-Meeting Track:** If you want to spread this session over two meetings, STOP here and close in prayer. Inform group members of the content to be covered in your next meeting.

### Start Option (10 minutes)

Begin your second meeting by having people form stand-up groups based on their positions in their childhood families: **If you were an only child, gather along the left side of the room. If you were the oldest child, gather on the right side. Middle children gather near the front and youngest children gather in the rear.** If any groups have more than six people, have them divide into two or more smaller groups. When groups are formed, invite people to share one thing they liked and one thing they disliked about their status in the family.

When groups have had time to share, ask for a show of hands of those who think only children had it best. Repeat for oldest, middle and youngest children. Probably, there will be a spread of responses. Lead into Step 3 by commenting, **Obviously, there are differences of opinion on this question. And we know from experience that in any grouping of two or more people, there is likely to be a great many areas in which we do not share the same opinions, ideas or feelings. That is why good communication skills are so vital to building and maintaining healthy family relationships in the face of the great diversity that exists within any family unit.**

Invite people to be seated.

### Step 3—Saying What I Feel (10 minutes)

Lead the group in quickly compiling a list of examples of positive things to say to family members. **Sometimes we fail to say helpful things because we simply don't think of them at the time. This exercise will give us a little practice in thinking of—and saying aloud—positive things we can say to build stronger relationships with our family members.** Show the transparency "Saying What I Feel," uncovering only the top item, "Affirm." Ask **What are some specific things we can say to affirm or praise someone in our families?** After a minute or so of suggestions, move on to the next item. Continue similarly through all six items.

As people share their ideas, push them to state their affirmations as they would really say them, avoiding the tendency to vague generalities. For example, if someone says, "I'd affirm her by complimenting how she looks," ask **Exactly what words would you use in complimenting her?**

### Option

This option will add 10 minutes to the Step 3 section.

Have people form pairs. Spouses should work together. Those who do not have a spouse at this session should work with another single person. Instruct one partner to choose "odds" and the other to choose "evens." Then each one puts one hand behind his or her back, and together they count "One, two, three." On "three," they show their hands and count the total number of fingers extended on both hands (0-10). If the total is an odd number, the person who chose "odds" will go first; if the total number is even, the other partner goes first.

Give these instructions to lead people in practicing positive communication one-on-one, again uncovering the transparency of "Saying What I Feel" one item at a time: **The partner who is to go first will be the parent. The other partner is the child. Parent, you have 30 seconds to affirm your child.** After 30 seconds, have partners switch roles and the new "parent" affirms the child.

Move to the next item (Be lovingly honest) on the transparency. This time have the role of spouses or other adult relatives. Again, they alternate, saying to each other specific things they could say to be lovingly honest with an adult family member. Continue similarly through the six items, alternating between communicating with a child and with an adult.

Conclude this exercise by inviting comments on what people liked and did not like about attempting to communicate positively with another person. Most likely, people will list as a negative the pressure of the activity (having to say something on the spur of the moment, especially with a time limit). Remind them that in real life, we often fail to say positive things when we are under pressure, so perhaps this exercise will make it easier to say the right thing when the situation arises.

## Step 4 Option—Nonverbal Communication Skills (15 minutes)

Point out that the impact of our communication is much more than just the words we say. Often, the way in which we say something is far more important than what we say. Ask **What are some of the factors in our communication that can add to or detract from the words we speak?** As people suggest ideas, list them on the chalkboard or a blank overhead transparency. Also, ask those suggesting ideas to tell how that particular factor contributes to the message being spoken: **Why does** (the expression on my face) **make a difference in how my message is received?**

After compiling a list of communication factors, ask volunteers to mention examples they have noticed in the group as others have been speaking: **When have you noticed someone in our group effectively** (using gestures) **to emphasize a point?**

Next, point out that we are often unaware of many of the factors that accompany our words. We tend to focus on what we want to say and our expression, our posture, our gestures, tend to flow along. An important aspect of nonverbal communication is that when we discipline ourselves to think about these factors, we become better able to control our emotional responses to people and situations. For example, the very act of intentionally moving close to a child and stooping down to eye level changes our emotional state from what it would be if we yelled our message from across the room or towered over the child. The obvious result of such actions is that, by taking actions that help control our emotional state, we are better able to focus on our message and on the person with whom we want to communicate, bringing about more effective, positive communication.

Ask **What are some specific actions we can take to help us reduce negative, conflict-producing emotions and enable us to be more self-controlled in our communications?** List the suggestions on the chalkboard or on a transparency.

# Getting Personal
## (10 minutes)

Instruct each person to choose one of the six positive communication examples noted from the story of David and Jonathan: Affirm, Loving honesty, Restraint, Listen, Express feelings, Encourage. **Select one that you feel you need to do more of in communicating with someone in your family.**

Allow a few moments for people to think and choose, then have everyone stand and find two or three other people who chose the same communication approach. Once everyone has found a group, give this instruction: **Starting with the person in your group who most recently laughed with someone in his or her family, explain why you feel you need to use more of the communication approach you just chose.**

After groups have had a few minutes to talk, give this next direction: **Now, starting with the last person in your group who just shared, turn to the person on your right and say something to encourage him or her to actually go home and start using this communication approach more often.**

### Getting Personal Option

This option will add 5-10 minutes to the Getting Personal section.

With people still standing, invite volunteers to share with the class a reason someone in their group gave for trying to increase their use of a particular positive communication approach. As reasons are shared, offer statements of affirmation or encouragement, both to help motivate people to actually do what they have discussed, and to provide examples of affirmation and encouragement (i.e., "Good thinking!" "I agree 100%, Sam." "Excellent reason, Cassandra." "I wish I'd thought of that.").

Close the session by inviting people to pray for someone in his or her small group, asking God's help in improving positive communication within that person's family.

Point out that the final topic of this series is exploring the connections between being part of God's family and an earthly family.

# Communication Barriers

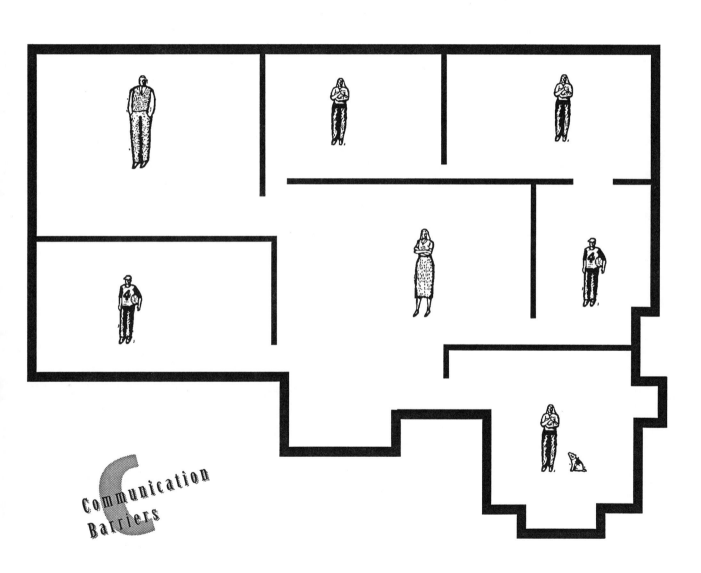

# Saying What I Feel

What could you say to:
Affirm a family member?

...........................................................................................................................................................

...........................................................................................................................................................

Be lovingly honest with a family member?

...........................................................................................................................................................

...........................................................................................................................................................

Show restraint in responding to a family member?

...........................................................................................................................................................

...........................................................................................................................................................

Listen to a family member?

...........................................................................................................................................................

...........................................................................................................................................................

Express feelings to a family member?

...........................................................................................................................................................

...........................................................................................................................................................

Encourage a family member?

...........................................................................................................................................................

...........................................................................................................................................................

# God's Family: Jesus Teaches Mary, Martha and Lazarus

## Session Keys

### Key Verses

"He came to that which was his own, but his own did not receive him. Yet to all who received him, to those who believed in his name, he gave the right to become children of God—children born not of natural descent, nor of human decision or a husband's will, but born of God." John 1:11-13

"How great is the love the Father has lavished on us, that we should be called children of God!" 1 John 3:1

### Key Idea

Successful families reflect God's love for each individual's unique qualities.

### Key Readings

Matthew 21:17; Luke 10:38-42; 23:44-49; 24:1-8; John 11:1—12:11

## Preparation

The house of Mary and Martha and their brother, Lazarus, was Jesus' home-away-from-home when in Judea. By noting His visits to these friends, we can learn some powerful truths about our own relationship with Jesus.

The two sisters in this family were obviously very different from each other. Martha was diligent, hardworking and willing to serve others. Practical, responsible, no-nonsense, take-charge—that was Martha.

In contrast, Mary was more introspective, more emotional, less concerned about appearances. And their brother? He seemed to quietly inhabit the background, being overshadowed by the two strong, individualistic women in his family.

So what do we learn from watching Jesus' visits to Bethany? First, we notice ready evidence of His love for these friends. He chose to spend time with them; He spoke honestly and lovingly to them; He affirmed them for their positive actions and attitudes.

Second, we observe that Jesus loved Mary, Martha and Lazarus just as they were, not demanding that they conform to a uniform pattern in order to earn His approval. At the same time, He loved Martha enough to encourage growth, pointing out an area to grow in.

And third, we recognize in reading these stories that Jesus loves us as He loved Mary, Martha and Lazarus. He loves each person as a unique, one-of-a-kind individual; and His love enables us to grow to our full, God-given potential. Through Him, we experience all the love and joy of being part of God's family.

Each person in your class has a special place in his or her own family. This session can help each one appreciate his or her own individuality, as well as the uniqueness of other members in their families, not just as interesting variations of humanity, but as God-given evidences of His creativity and love. Such an awareness is a significant foundation in making any human family a visible illustration of God's family—all those who have put their trust in God's Son, Jesus Christ.

Provide blank name tags and felt-tip pens. Wear a tag yourself.

Provide these materials:

Choice 1: At least 8 or 10 signs, mounted around the room (on walls, tables, floor, windows, etc.): "Favorite Dessert," "Favorite Restaurant," "Favorite TV Show," "Favorite Book," "Favorite Sport," "Favorite Breakfast," "Favorite Bible Story," "Favorite Vacation," "Favorite Park," "Favorite Vegetable," etc. For each person provide four or five blank index cards and a marking pen. Have ready masking tape and/or thumb tacks for mounting cards next to signs.

Choice 2: Have ready several pads of stick-on note papers (at least two inches square). Also have a supply of fine-tip felt pens. Divide the room in half, using a length of bright-colored yarn to mark the boundary. Place two signs on either side of the boundary, one lettered "Similar," the other lettered "Different." Leave an open area in the middle of the room around this dividing line.

Bibles, enough for each person to have a copy. Chocolate kisses or other small candies, enough for everyone.

Duplicate copies of "A Family Jesus Loved" on page 85 and "Sharing Our Faith with Our Family" on page 87, making one copy per person.

# Session 5 at a Glance

| SECTION | ONE-SESSION PLAN | | TWO-SESSION PLAN | WHAT YOU'LL DO |
|---|---|---|---|---|
| | 60 to 75 Minutes | More than 75 Minutes | 60 Minutes (each session) | |
| Getting Started | 10 | 10-20 | Session One: 20 | Introduce God's Family |
| Getting into the Word | 40 | 60-75 | 40 | A Family Jesus Loved |
| Step 1 | 10 | 15 | 15 | What a Family |
| Step 2 | 20 | 25 | 25 | Jesus and the Siblings |
| | | | Session Two Start Option: 10 | The Ugly Duckling |
| Step 3 | 15 | 20 | 20 | Sharing Our Faith with Our Family |
| (Step 4 Option) | (15) | (15) | 15 | Answering Hard Questions |
| Getting Personal | 5 | 10-15 | 15 | Prayer |

# Session Plan

## Leader's Choice

**Two-Meeting Track:** This session is designed to be completed in one 60- to 75-minute meeting. If you want to extend the session over two meetings and allow group members more time for discussion, **END** your first meeting and **BEGIN** your second meeting at the stop-and-go symbol in the session plan.

The boxes marked with the clock symbol provide optional learning experiences to extend this session over two meetings or to accommodate a session longer than 60-75 minutes.

# Getting Started

## (10 minutes)

### Choice 1—My Family's Favorites

Welcome people as they arrive and guide them to make (or find) and wear name tags. To help people continue to get acquainted and build relationships, give each person several blank index cards and a marking pen. Instruct them to wander among the signs placed around the room, and when they find a category for which their family has a definite favorite, they letter that on a card, plus their family name, and attach it next to the sign. Encourage them to talk with other people, comparing their choices with those of other families. If their family is definitely split in selecting a favorite in some category, suggest they tear a card in half and write down both options.

After most people have had time to "vote," invite people to be seated. Ask **Which category seemed to get the most entries? The fewest? The most diversity of choices? The most agreement?**

Introduce the topic for this session: **It's fun to notice that most of us and our families tend to have fairly strong, and often diverse, opinions about items that are not really matters of great importance. Today we are going to explore a dimension of our family lives that is of supreme importance to us as individuals and to the success of our families. We are going to look at the link between our human family and God's family.**

### Choice 2—Where Did That Come From?

Welcome people as they arrive and guide them to make (or find) and wear name tags. Point out the dividing line in the middle of the room and the two signs ("Similar" and "Different"). Give each person several stick-on notes and a marking pen. Instruct each person to letter on each note a way in which two or more family members are similar to or different from each other. Suggest a few categories such as musical tastes, athletic ability, sense of humor, appearance, hair color, disposition, political view and personality. Instruct people to place their notes on the floor on the appropriate side of the boundary, indicating the degree of similarity or difference by how close they put it to the line. For example, if two or more family members are just a little bit different in some category, place the note close to the line. If they are diametrically opposite each other, put the note far away from the line. Encourage them to compare their notes with those being placed by others. On the "Similar" side, the greater the similarities, the further away from the line the note should be placed.

When most people have had an opportunity to place a few notes, invite everyone to be seated. Ask **In light of the placement of these notes, how valid does the phrase "family resemblance" seem to be? On which side of the dividing line was it easiest to identify characteristics? Why? When a baby is born, why do all the rela-**

tives try to figure out who the baby looks like? What impact do these similarities and differences have on the functioning of our family units?"

Introduce this session's topic: One of the intriguing things about human families is that they are often used in Scripture in comparison with God's kingdom or family. God is often addressed as Father, and Jesus is referred to as His Son, largely because the parent/child relationship is something we all have experienced and understand. And we are often referred to as God's children in order to help us recognize the quality of the relationship we have with God and with each other. In this session, we are going to explore the link between our human families and the family of God.

## Getting Started Option: Find the Verse

This option will add 10 minutes to the Getting Started section.

Distribute Bibles to those people who need them. Divide the class into two or more equal-sized groups. Give this instruction: We're going to have a race. I'm going to call out a Bible reference that contains a statement about being in God's family. I'll then say, "One, two, three, Go!" and you are to start looking for that reference in your Bible. I'll repeat the reference once or twice while you're looking. As soon as you find it, raise your hand. The first team to have three people find the verse gets a point and that third person will read the verse aloud for all of us. At the end of the game, the winners all get wonderful treats for which I have spared no expense. Call out as many of these references, one at a time, as time allows:

Isaiah 64:8
Hosea 1:10
John 1:12
Romans 8:16
2 Corinthians 6:18
Galatians 3:26
Ephesians 2:19
1 Timothy 3:15
1 John 3:1

Mark each team's score on the chalkboard or a blank transparency. At the end, announce And the prize goes to...ALL OF US! As we've just seen in these verses, God has declared that all of us who put our trust in Jesus Christ are declared His children. To celebrate before we proceed with the rest of our study, here's a treat. Distribute the candy you provided.

# Getting into the Word

## (40 minutes)

### Step 1—What a Family (10 minutes)

Have people form at least three groups of no more than four or five people per group. Distribute copies of "A Family Jesus Loved." Assign one-third of the groups to focus on Mary, one-third to focus on Martha and the remainder to focus on Lazarus. Each group looks up the verses listed on the sheet and works together to write a brief description of its assigned person. Encourage the groups to use a little imagination, going beyond the few words in these verses to consider what they would expect this person to be like, including ways he or she was different from the rest of the family. The purpose is to make these familiar names come alive to us as real, flesh-and-blood people.

Allow five or six minutes for groups to read and write. Then invite volunteers from each group to read aloud their descriptions. On the chalkboard or a blank transparency, write below each character's name the key descriptive words each group uses.

After each group has shared, make this comment: **As with all families, Mary, Martha and Lazarus were not three peas in a pod. Just from the quick glimpses Luke and John give us, we get very definite impressions of three very different, unique individuals. It's not really important whether or not we have exactly pegged these folks. In fact, I rather imagine Lazarus eavesdropping on us and then going off to find the apostle John to complain. John could have taken a little more time to tell about Lazarus's career and his hobbies and his great sense of humor so that we'd have a better idea of what he was really like. What is really important, though, is that in recognizing the obvious differences between these three, we must note the words of John 11:5, "Jesus loved Martha and her sister and Lazarus." They did not have to all be alike in order for Jesus to love them.**

### Option

This option will add five minutes to the Step 1 section.

Invite people to recall the similarities and differences they noted earlier within their own families. Ask **How many of you have got at least one uniquely different individual living with you?** (All hands should go up.) **How many of you sometimes find, being human after all, that some of the ways another family member is different from you creates problems in your relationship with that person?** (Again, all hands should go up.) **Finally, in light of what you know about Martha, Mary and Lazarus and John 11:5, what impact do these differences make in how much Jesus loves the different members of your family?** (No difference at all!)

Lead group in looking at John 11:5, then have them read it aloud in unison, inserting their own names and those of their family members. **Some of us will get**

done reading sooner than others, but that's OK. If the first reading is a little weak, have everyone repeat it once or twice. You might encourage those with larger families to finish up a little louder to make up for the earlier finish by those with shorter lists.

## Step 2—Jesus and the Siblings (20 minutes)

With people in the same groups, assign the following verses for them to explore Jesus' responses to Mary, Martha and Lazarus. Look for what Jesus did to show His love for each particular person. Letter the verse assignments on the chalkboard or a blank transparency:

Mary: Mark 14:3-9; Luke 10:42; John 11:32-35

Martha: Luke 10:41,42; John 11:20-27,38-40

Lazarus: John 11:38-45; 12:1,2,9-11,17-19

Since we know that Jesus loved each of these people, and we can safely assume that He was well aware of each one's unique characteristics and needs, look for what Jesus did to show love to each one.

After five or six minutes, invite volunteers from each group to share what they learned. Expect answers to follow these lines:

Mary: Jesus affirmed her, and wept with her. He accepted her complaint that He had not been there to prevent Lazarus's death.

Martha: Jesus corrected and taught her. He accepted her complaint that He had not been there to prevent Lazarus's death.

Lazarus: Jesus restored Lazarus's life, then spent time with him, allowing Lazarus to stimulate the faith of many, and at the same time prod Jesus' enemies to the actions that resulted in Jesus' death and resurrection.

Make sure the point is made that loving someone does not always mean enjoying warm fuzzies. Sometimes we must patiently endure their outbursts and unjustified complaints. Sometimes we must correct or nudge a loved one into doing what we know is truly best.

Present the following lecture material to help people consider how Jesus' actions with Mary, Martha and Lazarus apply to our families today:

**1.** Recognizing that Jesus loves each individual in our families, and that He truly wants what is best for each one, what is the most loving thing we can do for the people we live with? Obviously, it is to share God's love with them, helping them experience that great love in their own lives.

**2.** In order to accomplish that for our families, what is the most important thing we must do? Obviously, it is to allow God's love to be real in our own lives. We can't simply tell our families that God loves them, nor even send them to places or people where they can learn about it. We must allow the love of Christ to transform our own lives so that in our daily encounters with our family members, that love will be there.

**3.** We don't have to be perfect representatives of Jesus Christ in order to effectively help our families grow in His love. We do have to be honestly seeking to grow in His love ourselves. Having seen that Jesus lovingly corrected Martha, we need to also be receptive to His corrections. Our family members can learn a great deal from seeing how we respond when we need to be corrected.

4. First John 3:1 tells us, "How great is the love the Father has lavished on us, that we should be called children of God!" Notice the superlatives here. First, God's love is referred to as "great," then we are told it has been "lavished" on us. And in what way is this great love given? By God welcoming us as His children. While none of us lives in a perfect family, we can all imagine the ideal family in which the perfectly wise Parent is completely loving toward each child. As we seek to grow as God's children, we become better able to lavish His love on our own children.

## Option

This option will add five minutes to the Step 2 section.

Read aloud John 1:11-13. Should there be any people in the group who have never made a personal response to receive Jesus Christ and become one of God's children, briefly share your own experience of coming to trust Christ as your Savior. Tell about the need you recognized in your life, how you came to believe that Christ could meet that need, and how your life has changed since that time. Lead the class in a brief prayer and offer to meet after class with anyone wanting to talk further or ask questions about becoming Christian.

**Note:** If you are completing this session in one meeting, ignore this break and continue with Step 3.

**Two-Meeting Track:** If you want to spread this session over two meetings, STOP here and close in prayer. Inform group members of the content to be covered in your next meeting.

## Start Option (10 minutes)

Begin your second meeting by briefly retelling the old fable of "The Ugly Duckling" in which a swan's egg got into a duck's nest and the young swan was mistreated by the ducklings for being different. Point out that the fable vividly expresses the very common fear of not belonging, of not fitting in. Ask **What are some other familiar stories or examples of a misfit, someone who is different from the rest of the family?** (Cinderella, Rudolph the Red-Nosed Reindeer, Joseph and his 11 brothers, "the black sheep of the family," etc.)

Comment: These stories are popular because the fear of not being accepted is so powerful that most children—and most adults as well—would rather be like the other ducklings now and give up the expectation of becoming a swan later. In fact, it is not at all uncommon to see talented and intelligent children purposely do poorly so they will not be seen as different from their peers.

Ask **How can a parent help an insecure child or adolescent learn to accept ways in which he or she is different?** Accept suggestions from volunteers, then ask **How impor-**

tant is parental acceptance of such differences in the child? (Obviously, it is of great importance.) Since we realize that parental love and acceptance of a child is so vital, what significance is there in realizing that our heavenly Father loves us just the way we are?

Accept comments, then continue with Step 3 and conclude the session.

## Step 3—Sharing Our Faith with Our Family (15 minutes)

Divide the room into three sections based on the age of peoples' children: Parents of preschoolers move to the right side of the room, parents of elementary-aged children go to the center, and parents of adolescents (middle school and up) go to the left side. Those who have children in more than one age group must choose which age group to explore. Instruct people to form groups of no more than four or five members per group within each section. Give everyone a copy of "Sharing Our Faith with Our Family."

Instruct the groups to share and write down ideas of specific things they can do to help their children learn about, respond to, and grow in a living faith in Jesus Christ. Point out that the focus is not on the parent having to become a repository of theological and biblical knowledge, but rather, it is on how the parent can help the child learn to know Jesus Christ in a personal way.

After four or five minutes invite volunteers from each section of the room to tell one idea they heard that they feel they can use with their children. Encourage people to write down any additional ideas they feel they may be able to use.

As time allows, share these guidelines:

1. Be honest. When you don't know, don't bluff. When you have doubts, admit them. Then share what you do know. ("I don't know how God can be everywhere at once. If I understood that, I'd be as smart as God, and you know I'm not that smart. I just know that God is so much greater than I can ever imagine.")

2. Teach by example more than by words. Our children are always watching, so intentionally do things in their presence that you want them to imitate. (Read your Bible when they're around. It might not be as conducive to contemplation as at other times, but if the Book is important to you, you need to let your children see you using it regularly.)

3. Talk about God in the middle of life. Don't relegate your faith to special times or days. Let your child see how faith in God touches all of life. (When something good happens, laugh and thank God. When trouble comes, bow and ask for help.)

4. Keep it simple. Avoid symbolic language and "jargon" as much as possible. ("What does 'bless' mean, Mommy?" "Well, dear, 'bless means...uh, it means...well, I'm not quite sure how to explain it." "Then why do you keep saying it?")

## Option

This option will add 10 minutes to the Step 3 section.

Invite people to ask questions about problems or situations that occur when seeking to teach children and teens about faith in Jesus. Invite others to share their experiences in response to someone's question. If someone makes a suggestion that seems "off-the-wall," invite other perspectives. Point out that every parent knows that each child is unique, and what works well with one child may be a total disaster with another. And what one parent can do successfully may be completely ineffective when done by another. When we recognize that God has created so much diversity and that He loves each unique individual, it frees us from the pressure of thinking there is one single right way to teach every child. While there are guidelines that cover a wide range of situations, there can be wide variety in how guidelines are implemented with different children and parents.

## Step 4 Option—Answering Hard Questions (15 minutes)

Comment: **Children are notorious for being able to ask questions that no grown-up can answer. And often, the younger the child, the more difficult the question, especially when it involves God or Jesus or prayer or other spiritual issues.** Select four to six parents who are recognized as being wise, consistent Christians. Ask them to sit facing the rest of the group as a "Panel of Peers." Explain: **Since none of us is far enough away from home to be considered an expert, and since many of us know each others' children and are well aware of our shortcomings, I have randomly selected these people, as veterans of the parenting challenge, to sit as a panel to tell us how they have answered or might attempt to answer some of the questions children tend to ask about matters of the faith.** Assure the panel that they can feel free to admit when a question stumps them, since one of the marks of good parenting is honesty. To help get things rolling ask a few typical questions such as:

Why can't I see God?
How does God hear me when I pray?
How can Jesus get inside my heart?
Is Jesus the same as God?
How do I know the Bible is true?
Why does God let bad things happen?
Why didn't God answer my prayer?

Invite others in the group to raise questions for the panel that their children have asked. If a question stumps the panel, invite others in the class to suggest possible answers.

In the last few moments, point out that when a child asks a one-sentence question, he or she expects a one-sentence answer. Just because a child has asked a question about a big issue, there is no reason to "dump the whole load" all at once.

A brief, simple answer is best, followed by asking, "What else would you like to know?" If the child's interest has been piqued, there will be additional questions. If the child's curiosity has been satisfied for the moment, that's all that need be done for the time being. The best answer is one that stimulates the child to want to know more, rather than one that saturates the child with more information than he or she can absorb.

# Getting Personal

## (5 minutes)

Invite people to form groups of four or five. Starting with the person in the group who most recently changed a light bulb at home, have each person ask the group, in 25 words or less, for prayer about one family-related concern. Next, the person to the left offers a one- or two-sentence prayer for the first person, then shares his or her request. Continue similarly around the group.

### Getting Personal Option

This option will add 5-10 minutes to the Getting Personal section.

After the groups have prayed, instruct them to continue around the circle one more time with each person sharing one thing he or she has gained from participating in this series: **Tell each other how being part of this group has helped you or will help you.** Be prepared to share a benefit you have gained from studying the content and/or being part of the group. Then allow the group members to share with each other.

Restate your offer to talk with anyone who would like to know more about becoming a Christian. Close in prayer.

# A Family Jesus Loved

"Jesus loved Martha and her sister and Lazarus" (John 11:5).

**What a Family**

Write a brief description of one member of Jesus' "adopted family":

Mary
Luke 10:38,39
John 12:1-3

Martha
Luke 10:38-40
John 12:1,2

Lazarus
John 11:1-3,35,36
John 12:1,2

.............................................................................................

.............................................................................................

.............................................................................................

.............................................................................................

.............................................................................................

.............................................................................................

**Jesus and the Siblings**

Mary

.............................................................................................

.............................................................................................

Martha

.............................................................................................

.............................................................................................

Lazarus

.............................................................................................

.............................................................................................

.............................................................................................

# Sharing Our Faith with Our Family

Things I can do/say to communicate my faith in God to my family are:

.........................................................................................................

.........................................................................................................

.........................................................................................................

.........................................................................................................

.........................................................................................................

.........................................................................................................

.........................................................................................................

.........................................................................................................

.........................................................................................................

.........................................................................................................

.........................................................................................................

.........................................................................................................

.........................................................................................................

.........................................................................................................

.........................................................................................................

.........................................................................................................

.........................................................................................................

.........................................................................................................

.........................................................................................................

*Sharing Our Faith with Our Family*